COURAGEOUSLY VULNERABLE

A PATH TO LOVING AND ACCEPTING YOUR 'IMPERFECT' SELF

JANA PRACKOVA

Copyright © 2021 Jana Prackova

First Edition- 2021

ISBN- 978-1-9993347-4-1 (Paperback)
ISBN- 978-1-9993347-5-8 (Ebook)
ISBN- 978-1-9993347-6-5 (Hardback)

Mystic Butterfly® is a registered trademark of Jana Prackova

www.mysticbutterfly.co.uk

Editor: Ellie Stevenson
Cover Illustration: Mgr. Maria Lezova
Cover Design: JD Smith Design
Interior Illustrations: Mgr. Maria Lezova
Interior Design: JD Smith Design

Disclaimer

This book is designed to provide information and inspiration to the reader. It is sold with the understanding that within this book, the author and the publisher are not engaged in providing specific legal, medical or other professional services. If such services are required, the reader is advised to contact an appropriate competent professional.

This is a work of creative non-fiction. It reflects the author's present recollection of the experiences over time. While all the stories in this book are true, some identifying details of the people have been changed to protect the privacy of those involved. The views expressed in this book are solely those expressed of the author.

Every effort has been made to ensure that this book is as complete and as accurate as possible. However, the book contains only information available to the author up to the date of first publication. Therefore, the text should be used as a general guide only and not as the ultimate source of information on the subjects covered.

The purpose of *Courageously Vulnerable* is to inspire. The author and publisher shall have neither liability nor responsibility to any person or entity with respect to any loss or damage caused, directly or indirectly, by the information contained in this book.

Contents

To my precious dad…thank you for everything in my life. You've left the earth too early and I miss you immensely, but my love for you will never fade away.

I love you with all my heart, forever.

'I wish I could show you, when you are lonely or in darkness, the astonishing light of your own being.'

Hafiz

INTRODUCTION

It was Saturday morning, 1.28 am. I was staring in the mirror in my hotel room in Hong Kong. That day, I realised how *broken* I still was. I hadn't slept at all the night before, I was spaced out due to jet lag, burnt-out and could hardly stand. My hair was dry and frizzy, and not looking great, unlike the last picture I'd posted on social media. My hands and feet were swollen, my face was red and my usual digestive issues were out of control. I looked sad. The feeling of unfulfillment was making me feel very weak and shaky. *What was I doing here?* I asked myself. Shortly after, the rest of the internal monologue continued: *you're always busy, always doing something, but you're not really living your purpose. You're a people pleaser and attention seeker, even though you claim you've passed that stage. You're not excited about life, you feel exhausted and you're still scared of everything. And most of all, your life looks good on the outside, but on the inside you're crushed, insecure and unhappy. What sort of life is this?*

I stood there, amazed, as if I'd just had a conversation with someone who'd been spying on me for years and had uncovered all the lies I'd been living and telling myself.

My life *was* a mess and this was the first time I'd

truly admitted it to myself. I finally realised that hiding behind the masks, covering up and adding colour to my less than ideal life was no longer going to work. There I was, teaching others about truth, yet not really living my own truth.

At the same time, I felt somehow liberated. This re-alisation made me more accepting of my imperfect self. As a side benefit, that moment also brought significant changes to my weekly blog and what I've shared with others ever since. The less than pleasant truth about myself somehow started feeling okay. At last, I began to feel more at peace, both with myself and with the world that surrounds me. I felt broken, but for the first time it was okay to admit it to myself, and step into my truth again, but this time more fully.

We all sometimes put on fake smiles, create false personas and wear different make-up for different occasions. But, for how long are we going to be able to keep on playing these games? How much energy do we still have left to be playing these roles and putting on these acts? One day, the world will find out, and most importantly, we will get fed up with this theatre perfor-mance, and the white lies will slowly, but surely, come up to the surface and eventually fade away. Then, we'll ask ourselves, how well did I really do? Was it worth the effort and time? Was it worth the agony, and the emotional terror?

My answer to these questions is: *yes!* You may have wasted years, but at the same time you've gained so much knowledge that no one can take away from you. Yes, you've put in so much effort, but at the same time this has taught you what works and what doesn't. Yes, you've been through agony, and maybe terror, but the experience has taught you some important lessons that can help you on your journey of personal and spiritual growth. You've learned from it.

I'm not going to lie to you. I feel hesitant, uneasy and unsure about what I'm about to share with you in this book. At the same time, I feel excited and somehow liberated. I'm full of hope that this book will become a catalyst of change for you, as I share my story with you, along with some of my deepest fears and secrets that I haven't told anyone before. Some people might think I have a wonderful life, but that's just their perception. The truth is, I don't. I'm still scared, sometimes anxious, unsure about my next step. But there's a big difference in my life right now. When I experience unpleasant emotions, I take a deep breath and say to myself: *it's okay*. I know the rainy days will pass, and the sun will shine, again and again. I've stopped being so hard on myself, because I know life is a journey and most of all, an exciting adventure, full of so many wonderful things, waiting to be experienced.

My intention is for you to stop being so hard on yourself too, wherever you are on your journey right now, or whatever you're currently going through. Simply own your current story and be okay with it, while you're learning how to love yourself, heal yourself and improve yourself. You're the most important person in your life. You deserve all that love, affection and energy you so freely give to others. Start filling your own cup first and only when you're overflowing, then you can become generous with your own precious energy. You may feel uneasy or insecure, or even a bit lost right now, and not knowing which way to turn. I'm here to tell you that you're not alone. If you have no one to talk to, let this book be your friend, your companion. Let it empower you, inspire you and bring moments of light into your life. Let it comfort you and motivate you, as you learn about my journey and what has helped me to rise above my challenges. And finally, let me show you how you can help and empower yourself too.

CHAPTER ONE

ADMITTING

Take a deep breath and breathe out. You're stepping on a journey to self-love and appreciation right now. This journey requires your full commitment. Are you ready? Yes? Saying yes is the first step to improving your wellbeing, even though you may feel insecure, lost and scared right now. That's okay. Not resisting, and simply feeling your present emotions is a pathway to healing and loving your imperfect self, and by imperfect, I actually mean your beautiful, unique and incredible self.

Learning to love yourself fully isn't always easy, but it is one of the best decisions you'll ever make. You owe it to yourself. It's time to let go of all the excuses and finally begin that interesting, exciting adventure. Now is the time to finally pause and re-evaluate your life, and search for its true meaning, its purpose and its mission. We all have one, no matter how insignificant our life might have felt up to now. Now is the time to put yourself and your needs first.

I used to be a people pleaser. Because I didn't have many friends, I would go out of my way to do favours for others, even though I knew they wouldn't do the same for me. I'm not saying there is anything wrong with doing favours for others, absolutely not. I love helping people. But there is a difference between doing favours from a place of love and really wanting to, and doing favours because you don't know how to say *No*, while your intuition is telling you, you shouldn't do it, but you still do it anyway and then you lose out and feel bad. The same also applies to getting easily talked into something, and then getting into trouble.

I was seeking the acceptance, approval, love and recognition I wasn't able to give to myself. I thought I wasn't good enough, that I was inferior and worthless. I was comparing myself to other people and falsely believed that their communication skills, education, social status, money or better clothes made them more special than me. They seemed to have lives so far away from the world I lived in, theirs were incomparable to mine. I was living in so much fear, denial and scarcity. My life was filled with much emotional turmoil and anger, and as a result of that, a lot of things in my life went wrong. My finances were off track, my overall wellbeing wasn't at its best and my soul was screaming for help and healing. My emotional wounds were still bleeding and were a long way from becoming scars, scars that would one day only be a reminder of how far I'd come, and how proud I was of myself.

The magic of admitting

Admitting to yourself that something in your life isn't working, isn't flowing is a huge deal. Many of us don't even realise that we're lying to ourselves on a daily basis. We become so part of these lies that they become second nature to us, and to our identity. This was the case for me. I remember years ago after I'd said several white lies over and over, to others and myself, how convincing they were. Others appeared to believe them, because at that point, they were so well rehearsed, and I hardly gave them a second thought. To summarise, I was living a lie, not only on the outside, but in my inner world too. I was living in denial. My vivid imagination was being used in a damaging ways, damaging to myself.

Becoming honest with myself was crucial. Only when I became honest with myself, could I also be honest with others. At first, I found it extremely difficult. I didn't want others to uncover the truth about me, so I continued to play the old game, for far too long, until I experienced an emotional breakdown at the age of twenty-three. Despite this, the lies and denial continued. I was feeling more crushed than ever before, but I still felt safer when I pretended, because I wasn't ready and didn't know how to let go of the fictional world I'd created. I wanted to, but I was stuck in a vicious circle I'd created, and somehow accepted. I was paying a huge price for it. It was like a maze, which didn't have an exit.

Pain, struggle, depression, anxiety and overwhelming fear were the only companions I had at this point in my life. As time passed, this maze was getting denser and denser and I was feeling more and more broken. I was screaming out loud but nobody could hear me through the barriers I'd placed around me. As a temporary solution, I would pour myself another glass of red wine, to ease the pain, as I did on most days at the time, even though it might be only 12 noon. By 2 pm the bottle would be gone. The wine lifted me up and numbed my unpleasant feelings of distress and anxiety, but it was fake. By 3 pm, I felt even more down and depressed than I had a few hours earlier. The feelings of worthlessness and anxiety deepened. This had become a repeating cycle that I practised every time I had an anxiety attack. I'm not particularly proud of this period of my life, but at the same time, I wouldn't trade it for anything. This dark period of my life taught me so much about myself, and most of all it gave me an opportunity to rise above it, and open the door to a happier and fulfilling life.

Do you live a lie?

Are you living a lie? Are you denying your true self? Are you ashamed of yourself and your story? Do you think you're not good enough? I used to answer a big YES to all of these questions. And there's nothing wrong with that. I admit it fully now, because being this way gave me an opportunity to become truly honest with myself. And, this is an opportunity to get honest with yourself too.

For now, I'd like you to do the following:

Get yourself a nice notebook, where you can write down your thoughts and express your feelings. If you have one handy now, perfect. If not, take a pen and paper and take some time to list the areas in which you may be lying to yourself. Then, later, you can rewrite this exercise in your new notebook.

It might go something like this:

'I post perfect photos on social media but my real life looks nothing like that. I look in the mirror every morning and don't like what I see. My hair looks unhealthy and I'm overweight.'

'I put on such an act every time I go to work, I feel disgusted with myself. Even though I don't particularly connect with any of my work colleagues, I pretend I care but the truth is, I don't. All I want is to get the day over, go home and hide from people.'

'I give advice to others as to what they should do to improve their lives, yet my life is a total mess. I feel like such a liar every time I do this, and I hate myself for it.'

This is an opportunity to get really honest with yourself and see that something isn't working. Once you admit what's going on, you can begin the healing process. First you have to feel these feelings, and only then you can start healing them.

I hope you will take the time to do this exercise, because it can be life-transforming. Admitting your true feelings to yourself and becoming honest, is an incredible shot of a healing potion, and is much better for you than pouring yourself a glass of wine or going shopping, to temporarily numb your pain.

The more potions like this you drink, the more healing you will experience. Aim to get all your insecurities, lies, daily dishonesties, *and* your real truth out on the table. When you have them all right in front of you, you can start doing something about them. Send them love, not judgement. Even though they may seem negative, they have served you all these years. They have somehow held you together, even though they didn't feel so good. They've helped you to function in the world, the best way you could. You did the best you could. At the time you didn't know any better and that's okay. All these things are still part of you, so they should be honoured, respected and treated with gentleness, because your whole being deserves to be treated that way. This process may feel uneasy, but in order to create change in your life, you need to become honest with yourself, and admit something isn't right and needs to be addressed. Only then can you start doing something about it.

I'm still feeling insecure in some areas of my life, I also feel afraid, but at the same time, I feel I'm more healed than ever before. Admitting and honouring all parts of me allowed me to send love and light to them, so they could start healing. The wounds that were bleeding could start forming scars which wouldn't be painful anymore.

It's your honesty that will move mountains and bring incredible shifts in your life. Don't be afraid to take this step. The healing that you can experience can be profound.

Am I saying that it's okay to be untruthful? No, but you lied to yourself and others, because up to this point you've believed it was the easier choice. Am I saying that it's okay to be fake? No, but there were and maybe still going to be moments in your life when you're going to be fake and that's okay. Am I suggesting you should say yes when you mean no? No, but there may still be many unhealed parts of yourself which will be prompting you to do this and that's fine too. There may be parts of you which are still deeply in fear and are making you act from a place of fear and insecurity.

Admit all this to yourself. Admit that you're still broken, still imperfect, still insecure even though you may be the chief executive of one of the most prestigious companies in the world. It's all okay. Nobody has it all together.

I'm officially announcing myself as the queen of imperfections and insecurity, the queen of inferiority and scarcity, even though I know, in truth, this isn't me. I'm admitting it all. Admitting my imperfections has been an enormous step for me, and for my soul's healing. It has been the first step to healing my inner being, my inner child who has been crying her eyes out, trying to navigate through this world, while being so confused and scared, and not knowing which way to turn. But she's still here *and* she's getting stronger and wiser. She's not so afraid now that she can't see the light at the end of the tunnel. Five out of ten times she takes a courageous decision forward, because she knows that when she takes that step, she'll step on another exciting journey, which will lead her even closer to her true self – the self which is always waiting to be discovered and can bring her closer to her completeness. She's no longer worried that she might never reach that completeness, because she knows as a human, she may never do so, and that's perfectly fine. She's no longer hard on herself for her past mistakes, because she knows they've shaped her and are constantly doing so, making her the person she's becoming. She knows she can improve and is improving daily, but at the same time she knows that when she fails, it's not the end of the world and she can begin again. With a new sunrise comes a new opportunity to uncover new possibilities for herself and her life. She's okay being her imperfect self and admits this happily to herself, and to the world.

CHAPTER TWO

ACCEPTING

When I was a little girl, I remember being made fun of by the kids in our village and at school. Someone from the village made up a nickname for me which stayed with me for many years, and some of the kids would address me that way, and did so for a long time. They didn't realise the effect this had on me, and on my self-esteem. After that, I trusted myself less, and was constantly looking for ways to hide, or to do something to be accepted. Even as I write these words now, my throat feels tight and tears are pouring down my face. I'm sitting in a café at the moment, so it's a little hard to hide in here, so I'm accepting how I feel and going with the flow. I'm accepting the moment I've been led to, and the reasons behind it. I want to share my experiences with you, with hope and a belief that they can inspire you, and perhaps shine a light on your life, so you can start seeing your own story from a different perspective.

Those kids calling me names, making fun of me and telling me I was stupid, without even getting to know me, was a soul-crushing experience.

There was also a group of very confident kids in our village whom everybody worshipped and wanted to be friends with. But I was scared of them. One day, when I was about twelve years old, when my sister and I were walking to the local shop to buy ice cream, I saw these kids walking towards us. My heart started racing, and I wanted to turn around, just to avoid them, but my sister told me to keep walking and just to ignore them. As they came closer, they started talking to each other very loudly, as if my sister and I weren't there, but their intention was to be as loud as possible, so we could hear their words. The conversation went something like this:

'*Can you see that* (the name they used to call me)? *She's* so *ugly and stupid. How could the girl walking beside her be her sister? It doesn't make any sense at all.*'

My sister told me, again, to ignore them. As we passed by, I burst into tears. What had I done to these kids for them to be talking about me like this? What had I done to deserve this? I'd never even been introduced to them. All this self-pity came up to the surface, as it always did, when someone did this to me. The early years of my life were filled with so much fear, worry and reluctance to be seen. Every day I kept wondering what I could do to be like the popular kids? How I could be accepted and be seen differently. I was lost, confused and felt unworthy. Living this way created an unhealthy imprint in my consciousness, making me feel I wasn't good enough as I was. This imprint was like a dark shadow, which has been following me around to this day. The good news is, now I'm fully aware of it, so every time I notice it, I question it and let it go before it does damage.

Approval seeking

The desire to be liked and accepted turned me into an unhealthy people pleaser and approval seeker. It created a lot of damage that was hard to live with and even harder to repair, years later. It took me years to shed old beliefs others had shared and I'd deeply accepted. I'm still working through these beliefs and learning to accept my imperfections, by honouring and loving them as they are. But it's the acceptance of myself that has brought light into my life. Learning to accept myself for who I am, has allowed me to recognise my worth and uniqueness. I've realised that my truth matters and that I deserve love and respect, like everyone else. Acceptance has healed many parts of my life, in the most magical way. Accepting yourself is an incredible gift you can give to yourself.

In my first book, *Mystic Butterfly: a guide to your true self*, I talked about how accepting my anxiety changed my life. I never talk about anxiety in great detail, because I'm not a health care professional, however, I occasionally share some of the lessons I'd learned and the personal realisations I'd had as a result of this experience. When I began accepting the feelings I was going through as part of me, instead of fighting them, my life began to shift and I started feeling more relaxed. The unpleasant feelings I was going through were part of me, and as they were part of me, I needed to co-operate with them, not fight them. When I fought, I was fighting part of myself, whereas when I accepted them, they became less threatening and less daunting.

Acceptance takes courage, but it's another step that will lead to your liberation and your connection to your truth. You'll be able to breathe more easily and your life will start to make more sense.

Acceptance, however, doesn't mean staying where you are and not working to improve your life. We should always be working on ourselves. What acceptance means is truly loving ourselves for who we are in this current moment in time, while working on making our lives better. Acceptance also means treating ourselves with love and respect, and giving ourselves credit for walking through this adventure courageously, despite our fear of what might lie around the corner. It means staying true to ourselves and honouring our unique journeys. We all want to be liked and accepted, but approval and attention seeking can lead us to disappointment and feelings of unworthiness. The truth is, you have nothing to prove to anyone!

Just the other day, I was thinking about how to inspire my beautiful community on social media and a lovely idea came to me within minutes. I immediately created a beautiful visual collage with some powerful words and was ready to share it on social media. Then, suddenly, a particular person came to mind, someone I believed would raise their eyebrows at my post and would think: '*There we go again. More of Jana's inspiring, self-help stuff!*' At that moment I began doubting myself and questioning the beautiful, inspiring message I'd been excited to share just a minute ago. I decided not to post it. An hour went by and then I thought: *Isn't that interesting? Why do we care so much about other people's opinions, and seek their approval to the extent that we begin to doubt ourselves and our creativity?* In the end, I posted the inspiring message anyway and let the self-doubt fade away. I learned another big lesson from this: I realised how much energy I was still wasting on worrying about what other people thought of me. It also made me see how much I still cared about others' opinions and how I was still unsure of myself. But why did I care? And why should anyone else's standards matter? Was I worse than anyone else? Of course not. This made me wonder why we do this to ourselves? Why are we striving to be so likeable, giving all these people, especially the ones who don't really know us, so much of our precious time and energy?

I understand now that it's because of the imprints we've been carrying around since the time we came to this world. It's the beliefs and programming we've received. But this doesn't mean we're victims of our conditioning. Not at all. Instead, we should look at this as an opportunity to give ourselves more love and acceptance, which we truly deserve. Then, we wouldn't give others so much space in our minds and seek the external approval that we could've done without in the first place. Instead of rejecting our beautiful selves, we should ask ourselves: *What is this going to cost me?* And, if the answer is denying your true identity, then we should let it go in an instant.

When we're trying to push something away, something we no longer want in our lives, we can feel a lot of resistance. This can feel overwhelming and frustrating. When I used to suffer from anxiety, I used to dread and fight these unpleasant emotions. I didn't want to feel anxious. I didn't want to feel uneasy. Who would? But one day, I discovered that when I accepted what I was currently going through was okay, this allowed me to feel more at ease. When I accepted the feelings, I wasn't as tense or in a constant fight or flight mode anymore. I realised that obsessing about the physical symptoms I was going through wasn't going to help me. Instead, I accepted these symptoms in that particular moment in time, accepted them as part of me. As they were part of me, they didn't need my judgement, but rather my love and compassion. This is what acceptance truly means. To go even deeper, let me share with you a simple meditation that can help you start the process of acceptance right away.

You have always been enough (meditation)

For many years I thought I wasn't good enough. Beginning the process of accepting and loving myself for who I was, became life-transforming.

Allow the following meditation to bring love, peace and comfort into your life.

Please read it first, then do the visualisation exercise. You can access the pre-recorded visualisation/meditation on my website: www.mysticbutterfly.co.uk/meditation

Find a comfortable place where you're not going to be disturbed for at least ten minutes. Close your eyes to avoid any visual distractions. Become aware of your breathing. Breathe in slowly and deeply. Take a few deep conscious breaths like this and then return your breathing to its natural flow.

Now, I would like you to visualise that you're walking in a beautiful meadow full of daisies. The sun is gently caressing your face with its warm rays. You are spreading your arms wide and appreciating the moment you're in. You're absorbing the positive energy that is surrounding you and you're feeling happy to be alive, to be breathing, and just being in this beautiful moment. There is nothing else you need right now. You're happy, just as you are. You're enough because you are you. Being you is a reason for celebration. There is nobody like you and there's never going to be. How wonderful it is to know this? Your perfectly imperfect self is enough, and that's all that matters.

Now, repeat after me:

I love and accept myself for who I am. I approve of myself. I am enough. I have always been enough. I have nothing to prove to anyone. I love this interesting, sometimes crazy adventure called life. Accepting my imperfect self is one of the greatest gifts I have ever given to myself. I am loveable. I am true to myself. My feelings matter and I express them honestly. I am who I am. I am beautiful in my own unique way. There is no one like me and there is never going to be. It is safe to be myself. It is okay to be scared sometimes. It is okay to feel uncertain. It is okay not to know what's around the corner. I am excited about my future, even though I feel nervous about it. I am grateful for this amazing life. All is well.

You're still standing in the middle of the beautiful meadow full of daisies. You're at peace with yourself. You are okay, even though you don't know what tomorrow brings. You accept the moments as they come and you're ready to carry on, on this interesting journey called life.

When you're ready, become aware of your surroundings, of your body, stretch a bit if you like, take a slow, deep breath and when you're ready, gently open your eyes. Take your time getting back up.

Afterwards, have a glass of water to purify your body.

I believe that this meditation can begin the process of accepting your beautiful self a little more today. Remember, this work can be a lifetime process, so relax into it. I'm still learning to accept parts of me that can't be changed and also parts of my personality that I didn't even know existed, and that I'm only discovering now. I'm going with the flow and I'm doing the best I can in every single moment of every single day. I'm still scared, very scared at times, and I'm unsure what tomorrow will bring, and that's okay too. On top of that, I'm deeply grateful for this amazing journey I'm able to experience, and I'm continuing on it with so much love and grace, even though I'm full of uncertainty. All is well and life is unfolding as it should.

CHAPTER THREE

FORGIVING

A few years ago my world fell apart, when a friendship, which I'd valued and respected, ended unexpectedly. I won't go into too much detail, to protect this person's identity, but I learnt a number of lessons from this interesting experience. When the friendship ended, I felt crushed, very sad and I was crying a lot. It took me weeks to get back to normal, which I did, thanks to the amazing support of my boyfriend and my wonderful family. I distracted myself with work, not wanting to think about what had happened, and numbed my emotions, pretending everything was fine. The truth was, I wasn't fine. I was missing my friend, who I knew wasn't coming back. At the same time, I was angry at how the situation had been handled, and I felt I hadn't been treated fairly.

A few weeks went by, then I made the decision to take responsibility for my part in the separation, and began to accept that this person was meant to leave my life, to make space for someone new to come in, someone who really wanted to be my friend. Accepting this was very comforting, but there was still something missing. I could still feel energetically attached to this person and I needed to let go. I tried many techniques I'd learnt throughout my spiritual training and development, but these only gave me temporary relief. I believe this was because I was holding onto so much resentment towards this person. I needed to go deeper. Then, one day, while sitting in meditation, I asked for spiritual guidance on how to let go of this person. An answer came to me. It was to forgive. At first, I was angry. *I* wasn't the one who should be forgiving, *I* hadn't done anything wrong. But then I remembered that forgiving someone doesn't mean agreeing with how they might have treated us. It simply means not allowing that person or a situation to control our life anymore, on an energetic level. Forgiveness means letting go gracefully. I set on a path of becoming willing to forgive this person. It wasn't easy to start with, but I didn't give up. I started seeing this person as me, feeling the same. Being scared, doing their best in any given moment, being uncertain and unsure of their choices, and working towards fulfilling their dreams in this scary but beautiful world. I was able to see this person in their light, as well as in their darkness, and this allowed me to see the whole situation from a different perspective. It was life-transforming, and incredibly liberating at the same time. The foggy feeling I'd been carrying with me for some time, started lifting and forgiveness started setting in.

In this chapter we're going to learn the true meaning of forgiveness, whether that's towards ourselves or others. We are going to look at the blessings that forgiveness brings.

It is important to ask ourselves: *'Do I want to stay imprisoned in my past, in the situations that can't be changed or do I want to free myself?'*

The past is not here anymore and there's nothing that can be changed about it, but our approach to the past *can* be changed. Once we stop carrying our past mistakes, situations and people into our present, then we can build a better future for ourselves. The present influences the future. We're creating our future through our present choices.

The true meaning of forgiveness

If I had to talk to you about all my past mistakes I could write a trilogy. They'd make an interesting novel, for sure. First and foremost, I want you to know that your past mistakes don't define you, nor do your past experiences. So put your beautiful mind at ease right there. When you start forgiving the past, you'll begin creating different present experiences, and as a result of that, a better future for yourself. Dwelling on something which isn't here anymore and can't be fixed is a waste of time and energy. So why do we do it?

In chapter two I mentioned a group of kids who picked on me and made fun of me when I was younger. Yes, it was unpleasant, and unfair. And yes, it crushed my confidence. But now, I've forgiven all of them, and the others who hurt me so deeply at a vulnerable stage of my life. These days, when I travel back home to Slovakia, I sometimes see some of these people. They still live in the village, and some of them are married and have children. They always say '*hi*' to me and I smile and I say hello back. I suspect, when they see me, they feel a bit embarrassed because of what happened all those years ago. I sometimes want to tell them not to worry about it anymore, and that I've forgiven them. But at the same time, I don't want to revisit these experiences again. It would also feel a bit awkward, because we have nothing to say to each other. I hope they feel I've forgiven them. I know when we're children we don't always understand the effect our words can have on others, especially on other children, and how much they can hurt.

When we do a deeper forgiving work, I believe the people we're forgiving can feel it on a soul-level too, even though we don't talk to them anymore. This is the beauty of true forgiveness. You don't have to be friends with such people, but by forgiving them, you're taking their power to control your life away. This also applies to people you haven't spoken to for years. Holding grudges and resentment towards someone is a form of control, and it gives your precious power away. To forgive, as mentioned above, doesn't mean you agree with what they did to you. It's simply setting yourself free.

Forgiving yourself

We often don't realise that we have a lot of forgiving to do, including forgiving ourselves. Forgiving ourselves for our past mistakes, for the unwise choices we made, for not speaking up, for acting from a place of fear, for being untruthful to ourselves and others, for being too loud or too shy, too needy or too... – you fill in the blank.

Forgiveness is not an easy process, but it's definitely one that will set us on the path to freedom and to more fulfilment in life. By forgiving yourself you'll feel an enormous weight being lifted off your shoulders. You'll be able to see more clearly, to breathe more easily and your life will feel somehow lighter, happier and more meaningful. When you forgive yourself, you'll acquire the courage to also forgive others. So, let's have a look at how you can start forgiving yourself today.

For the next fourteen days (or longer if you wish), recite this statement every morning and every evening, or as often as possible: *'I forgive myself for my past mistakes. I've learned from them.'* You can also write the statement on a piece of paper, and place it on your mirror or vision board as a reminder that you're in the process of forgiving yourself. This way, you're also going to see it in front of you every single day. Repeating this is not deluding yourself. It's simply acknowledging that you're ready to let go of something you have no control over anymore.

Life is a huge learning experience. We're all learning and growing as humans, and also as souls. We make choices based on our current knowledge and under-standing. We may not be proud of some of our past choices, but we can always forgive ourselves, and at the same time be grateful for the powerful lessons that we've acquired from these 'unwise' choices. So, forgive yourself today for not knowing all the answers. Forgive yourself today for not being true to yourself. Forgive yourself for saying yes when you meant no. Forgive yourself for talking to others in a way you may regret now – if you'd known better then, you would've done better. Forgive yourself for judging yourself and others. Forgive yourself for blaming yourself and others. Forgive yourself for denying the truth of who you really are. Forgiving yourself gives you permission to rise above the past and to tune into the truth of who you really are.

Forgiving others

Forgiving others means not letting the people or situations from your past control your life anymore. Although it's not always easy to forgive, doing so sets you free. You're not forgiving someone for them but for yourself, and for your own peace of mind. Forgiving someone doesn't mean you have to associate with them in the future. Not at all. You're forgiving them because you want to move on with your life and stop letting past experiences control you. This way, you can focus your precious energy on the things that really matter to you.

To forgive someone, first of all, you have to be *willing* to forgive, as *Louise Hay* suggests in her book, *You Can Heal your Life*.

Secondly, taking responsibility for your part in the situation/experience is required. And if that means recognising that a person who wronged you doesn't deserve a place in your life anymore, that's fine. But taking responsibility for your part also means acknowledging *your* mistakes and looking at the situation from the other person's point of view.

When you're not ready to forgive

Not being able to forgive doesn't make you a bad person. Sometimes, you're not ready to forgive, yet. In time you might be, so the practice until then would be: *Let it be*. Let the experience stay in the past and stop revisiting it. At the same time, be kind to yourself and don't let your mind wander to places you don't want to give your energy to. Focus your attention on the present moment, because that's the only place where true life exists. When the time is right, then forgive. I think you'll know when you're ready. You'll feel it. Go with your intuition.

It's not always easy to forgive, but the liberation that comes with it can open many doors for us. As I've mentioned, I've been through my fair share of hurts, break-ups and disappointments. But what I've learned from these experiences has been priceless. Now I know that holding onto such situations or experiences won't make my life any better, but rather more miserable. In contrast, shifting my awareness and becoming *willing* to forgive, brought many blessings and magical healing into my life. The beautiful thing that I learned through forgiveness work is that I always have a choice. I can hold on to the past or I can let it go. Now I know that it's safe to let go, it's safe to forgive. I'm very grateful for the lessons I've learned along the way. They helped me, and shaped me to become the person I am today. I know that I deserve a happy and fulfilling life, so I made a decision to break the spell, and became willing to forgive myself and others, and set myself free. You too have that choice, so choose wisely and unchain yourself and your beautiful soul from the past, which is not its place of residence, but only a place of reference. You deserve a beautiful life. Set yourself free.

A letter to the people who have hurt me

Many things happen throughout our life: good, bad, exciting or challenging. People come into our lives, then they leave, sometimes, even without explanation. I've experienced this many times. People have hurt me and turned their backs on me, often when I've needed them most. Like I said before, I could write pages about my past hurts, disappointments and sadness. Most of us could. I now understand that some people come to our lives for a lifetime, and others come to play shorter roles. But every single person can become our teacher, if we choose to see them that way.

I believe that writing a letter to the people who've hurt us in the past can be very therapeutic, and a liberating experience. This letter isn't for them, it's for you. Perhaps to get the closure you never got, to express the feelings you never had a chance to express. To say the things you were too afraid to say out loud. To say how you really felt. I'd like to share with you a personal letter addressed to the people who've hurt me. I've decided to include it in this book to inspire your own forgiveness process. I'm not suggesting you should share your own letter publicly too. That letter is for you and your own healing journey. The letter I'm sharing with you is a generic letter. It doesn't contain anything too specific or negative, but it focuses on the lessons, and the good things which came out of my disappointments. Let this letter be an example for you to start your own liberating process, freeing yourself from past hurts. Thinking and worrying about the past has been holding you back from living the life you desire. Release the ex-boyfriends or girlfriends, former friends, past employers or any random strangers who you feel have treated you wrongly or unfairly. I believe that everything in life is a choice. Let's make a choice right now to step out of the victim-zone and take full responsibility for our lives and our choices. Worrying and replaying hurtful old memories in our minds will only keep us stuck in the past forever. You deserve inner peace, and the chance to release that difficult past, permanently.

Here is my letter

Dear ex-partner, former friend, colleague and anyone who has hurt me,

Thank you for the lessons I've learnt from you. I understand that the reason we were part of each other's journey, was because at the time our energies matched. After a while, having gained more of life's experiences, we stopped being on the same frequency and as a result, we went our separate ways.

Unfortunately, the ending of our journey together wasn't ideal. We didn't say goodbye to each other and wished each other good luck with our next venture. But I know that our friendship/relationship has served its purpose, and now it's time to move on to something else, something new and exciting. It's time to let go and get ready for the next chapter.

I want you to know that I take full responsibility for my part, and for everything I've ever said or done while we were in each other's lives. I don't blame you for anything. Thank you for the lessons and thank you for the experiences, even though some of them were very painful and I once wished they'd never happened. I now believe I had to go through them, but that you had to go through them too. Let's make a decision today, to cut the cords which are still keeping us attached to each other, and in some way holding us back. Let's release the tension, the blocks and the history between us. Let's cut them once and for all, so we can start focusing on the future that awaits us. Life is too short to be unhappy, and holding onto old resentments and unpleasant memories doesn't make sense. Let's start investing our precious time on this planet in things that are happy and exciting.

If you've recognised yourself in this letter, please know that I've forgiven you, or am in the process of doing so. When I look at both of us from a higher perspective, I see us as beautiful souls, beings of love and light. When I see us this way, I completely understand why we had to go through this, no matter how painful our story might have been. You and I had to learn these lessons to understand something important, something which may be revealed to us later. These lessons needed to be learned to help us with our personal and spiritual growth, even though they've caused hurt and disappointment to both of us.

So, have a beautiful life, dear friend. Gain as many experiences as you possibly can, and most importantly, enjoy this beautiful adventure called life. I wish you only the best on your own unique journey.

With love,
Jana

Nobody comes to our life as a mistake. Everything is happening for our highest good, and there is a universal message in every relationship we encounter. Learn the lessons and enjoy your adventure. Forgiving yourself and others is a beautiful gift you can give to yourself. Don't hesitate any longer – start this liberating process today.

CHAPTER FOUR

HEALING

Jenny is 35 and lives in London. She is single and works for a well-known fashion magazine. She has a beautiful figure and long blond hair. Her pretty wide green eyes reflect her wisdom and a kind nature. She sends out the vibe of a goddess, a mysterious energy that is very attractive.

On the outside, Jenny seems to have it all. She is stylish, beautiful, successful and admired by many, but on the inside she feels lonely and sometimes lost. Every time she falls in love with someone, she gets heart-broken. People are often surprised when she tells them she is single, always single. What keeps Jenny happy and fulfilled are her amazing hobbies.

She takes acting classes three times a week. She's very serious about acting and believes that one day she'll be a movie star. She does amateur acting at her local theatre too. It's a friendly place full of nice people of all ages. One of the fellow actors there is Gareth, a thirty-four year old Welsh architect who moved to London a couple of years ago. Jenny has been secretly in love with him for a few months now. Sadly, for Jenny, Gareth is in a relationship with another woman. Jenny loves Gareth, but she's not ready to tell him yet how she feels. She wants him to be happy. His relationship with the other woman seems serious. Jenny often says: *'You can't really choose who you fall in love with. It just happens.'* Jenny wouldn't want to interfere with or break up this relationship, so she suffers in silence, keeping her emotions inside. Unrequited love is very familiar to Jenny. She has experienced it far too many times. As strange as it may sound, it feels good to be in love anyway. Maybe she's hoping, deep within herself, that this platonic love will one day turn into a real love and that everything will be perfect. Miracles and magical surprises do happen and Jenny believes in them.

Gareth and Jenny have a lot in common. They're both actors, they love adventures and adore Shakespeare's work. Recently, the whole theatre group went to Stratford-upon-Avon, Shakespeare's home town. They loved every minute of it. They wore *Shakespearean* costumes and even played Romeo and Juliet. And guess who was Romeo, and who was Juliet? No surprise, then.

Jenny often cries. A good romantic film, an inspiring book, someone who touches her heart... she gets very emotional. Jenny doesn't mind. Crying washes away her sorrows and she feels better afterwards. Once, a psychic told her that she is an old soul who feels people's pain and emotions, and is very sensitive to them. When she cries she lets out the emotions she's absorbed from others.

At times, life can be monotonous for Jenny. Work, home, study, sleep, then work again. Even though she likes her job, lately it's become more routine and she's ready for a career opportunity. Recently, an interesting audition came up for Jenny and she did a great job. She's currently waiting for a decision on whether she'll get a role in a film with some brilliant prospects. This could be her big break. She feels excited and nervous at the same time.

Then, Jenny decides to tell Gareth how she feels about him. She has been thinking about taking this step for a while and has finally found the courage. It wasn't an easy decision, but after listing many reasons why she shouldn't tell him, she found one why she should. She deserves true happiness, and holding on to something which she may only be wondering about isn't healthy. She faces her fear and tells Gareth how she feels. To cut a long story short, Gareth very gently reveals to Jenny that he's just got engaged to his girlfriend. Jenny gives him a hug and says that she's genuinely happy for him with tears in her eyes. Of course, she wants him to be happy. When you truly love someone, you want the best for them even if it's not in your favour. Gareth doesn't like to see Jenny upset like this, but there's nothing he can do. His heart belongs to someone else.

Jenny, being familiar with the feelings of a broken heart, goes home and cries all night. Tears always wash away her pain, and after a while this allows her to see clearly again. The following morning, she remembers a past experience when she took a leap of faith and travelled across the world to visit someone she met on the internet. She really liked this person and wanted to know if the liking was real. This actually happened twice to Jenny. Jenny falls in love easily, but yet again, the love was only platonic and unrequited. One time, she went all the way to New Zealand, the other time to Hawaii, only to find out that these guys didn't feel as she did. She felt distraught for a while, but as time passed, her wounds began to heal. Now, Jenny pulls herself together, as she always does. Remembering these stories gives her strength and hope. She realises that, no matter what, she'll be okay and will get over Gareth too. She also knows why her previous relationships didn't work out. She always notices the lessons she learns from any experience and recognises the great wisdom behind them.

A week later, something exciting happens. Jenny lands her first major role in the film she auditioned for. Even though she's heartbroken and still thinks about Gareth, she's happy and ready to focus on her promising new acting career. They want her to start in a couple of months. It will be her day job for some time. Jenny gives notice at her present job at the magazine. She's been ready to do that for a while now. Acting is her passion and that's what she wants to pursue.

Despite her romantic misfortunes, Jenny will continue to fly high and keep radiating her goddess-like energy everywhere she goes. She knows this energy has also brought her the role in the film, and who knows, may make her a star. She knows this already without needing other people's approval or validation. She's strong and independent and understands that even though things don't always work out exactly as she'd like them to, there's always something magical waiting for her around the corner. Jenny knows life is an exciting adventure, which should be celebrated in her own special way, and for this wonderful gift from the Universe she'll always be grateful.

This story isn't about Jenny, but about me. I wrote it a few years ago when I was heart-broken and it pretty much summarised my life up to then, even though the story is unique in itself. Deep down, we all know that we're good enough, yet we still idolise others and place them ahead of us, acting in a needy way, and leaving our beautiful selves in the background. It happened to me many times until I learned some powerful lessons, through pain and struggle.

When I was younger, I didn't love and accept myself for who I was. I was constantly comparing myself to other people, trying to be more like them instead of being myself. I was putting other people's needs before mine, as if I didn't matter. Saying yes, when I meant no was attracting people into my life who would intentionally and even unintentionally be taking advantage of me. My energy attracted them. I didn't have boundaries and didn't understand what it meant to be assertive. As I've already mentioned, I'd go out of my way to do favours for others, even though I knew they wouldn't do the same for me. I sought acceptance and approval and that was all that mattered. I idolised other people based on their education, looks, social class and a job title. I was young, lost and insecure.

Where did this come from?

It was 1992, the summer and a school holiday. I was playing outside our house in Slovakia, with one of my friends. We were playing a game and she wanted to go first. She always went first, and I was fed up with it, so I asked: *'Can I go first today?'* But she got upset and said if she couldn't go first, she was going home. She started walking away. To make her stay and keep the peace, I said: *'Please, don't go,'* and of course, I let her go first in the game.

This story is a clear example of how my people pleasing and approval seeking behaviour began. From then on, I acted as if everyone else was more important than me, and in everything: relationships, work and friendships. I'd developed a soul-crushing habit.

In my mid-twenties I started to realise what I was doing, but by then the habit was hard to break. Putting myself first was something I've never done before, and self-love and acceptance weren't in my dictionary. But for the first time I'd started noticing that something wasn't right and that something needed to be done about it. At the same time I was suffering from anxiety. My anxiety was so bad I was panicking several times a day. I also developed a slight addiction to alcohol, which I found very hard to let go of. I've never really opened up about my alcohol addiction before, not even in my previous book. It was mostly a side effect of my anxiety. When I was anxious, then had a drink or two, I began to feel more relaxed. Of course this was only temporary, but the discovery led to a very bad habit which was difficult to let go of.

The drinking always started very innocently, with one or two drinks, but later on, I was relying on alcohol to calm me down on a daily basis. Every time I'd feel a panic attack approaching, I'd reach for a bottle of wine, or run to the supermarket to buy one. Even though the alcohol gave me temporary relief from the feelings of hopelessness and my fear of going mad, the feelings became twice as worse the next morning, with the hangover. And what would I do to numb those even worse feelings? I'd have another drink. So now I'd got into another vicious circle which it was difficult to get out of. After living this way for a while, I realised it wasn't living, simply existing. I knew I couldn't carry on like this for much longer.

You may be wondering why I didn't seek medical help to help me with my issues? I did. Many times I found myself in an emergency room hyperventilating, thinking that I was having a heart attack or that I was going to pass out and die. Living this way was frightening. Beside the emergency room visits, I also had counselling sessions and regular visits to the doctor. Medical professionals offered me some sort of relief and reassurance every time and I was extremely grateful for it, but I also knew I had to help myself. First of all, I had to let go of the alcohol for good.

Was it easy? No. Alcohol was my safety blanket, strange as that may sound. I never really *liked* alcohol, neither the smell nor the taste. What I did crave was the temporary relief it offered me – from my feelings of going mad. When I stopped relying on alcohol every time I felt an anxiety attack approaching, it wasn't easy.

I would often find myself halfway to the supermarket, ready to buy another bottle, then I would pause, realise what I was doing and go home. The setbacks were awful, but I've never touched a drop of alcohol since that decision, one of the best I've ever made. I'm happy to say that I've been sober for over a decade now. But letting go of one bad habit made more develop, from food addiction to not eating properly and getting too thin. There were others such as addiction to exercise, social media or unhealthy relationships. By this point, I was fully aware of what was happening and when something similar happens now, which sometimes still does, I take a similar approach to the one I took with alcohol. If you're struggling with an addiction of any kind right now, please do seek medical advice. The medical professionals can definitely offer you lots of support and direction.

As tough as it was, going through my anxiety issues, addictions, people pleasing and approval seeking behaviour led me to the road of self-love and acceptance. And truth to be told, I'm very grateful for all these experiences. If it wasn't for them, then maybe I'd be a different person today.

Guilt and shame

When I began looking after myself more, starting to put myself first and living a healthier lifestyle, there was another side effect: guilt and shame. I was no longer using my safety blankets to avoid feeling my real feelings and this led to lots of guilt and shame in my life.

Guilt and shame for my past actions became ever-present and prompted me to take a detour into feeling not good enough. Even though I wasn't using substances anymore to stop the pain, I still used my imagination in a damaging way to feel good about myself. I couldn't accept myself for who I was, so I'd create stories and a false persona, one who'd appear good on the outside but was actually broken and so lost on the inside. Replacing my true self with false images of who I was, was painful, but seemed like an easier and safer choice at the time. After a long period of living in this confusion, I exhausted myself to such an extent that I had trouble functioning on a daily basis, and reached another bottom. I realised that sooner rather than later I needed to escape this silly game. When I finally made that decision, it was liberating, but it also came with even more feelings of guilt and shame. By learning to accept myself for who I was, one day at the time, an emotional healing began taking place.

Break the old, build the new

A beautiful shift in my life occurred once I'd made the choice to see myself beyond all the imperfections I believed in, and thought I should be hiding. My healing journey is an everyday process and it continues even as I write these pages. As I'm aligning more and more with my true self every day, many old wounds are coming up to the surface. The funny part, which isn't always so funny, is that they often appear at the most unexpected times. They come up in the moments when I feel that

I'm finally on the right track and life is good. But as unpleasant as they may seem, I'm fully committed to clearing them, one at the time as they show up.

Sometimes in life, we reach a point where everything seems to be going against us, especially when we finally begin to take a path towards true healing. We may feel that everything is falling apart. In moments like this, it's important to remember that in order to create something better for ourselves, the old needs to fall apart, so we can rebuild ourselves. I know this can be scary and uncomfortable, and it hurts an awful lot. But it's also part of our healing process. You may not understand the reason behind those challenges right now, but you can learn to trust your journey anyway. This is a path to your truth, and many blessings will be revealed to you later in life, when the time is right.

I know that I'm slowly, but surely cleaning up my side of the street and the damage I caused to my beautiful self, in those thirty-something years on this planet. I want to do my very best to be as true to myself as I possibly can. I want to stop being so hard on myself and I know that if I fall, I'll get up and do my best, again and again for the rest of my life. Dealing with guilt and shame isn't always easy, but there are things we can do to start healing and transforming them.

The art of being vulnerable exercise

When you are healing on an emotional level, becoming vulnerable is crucial. I call being vulnerable an art. You are learning to express your true feelings, just like an artist painting a picture that is being channelled from deep within their soul.

Get your notebook and a pen and think about in which areas of your life you could become more loving and accepting of yourself? In which ways are you not giving yourself the love and respect you desire and fully deserve? Are you resenting any part or parts of your body? Are you resenting any side of your personality? Is there any area of your life where you could be braver, more outspoken and more true?

Go back in time and think about any experiences you've had which encouraged you to think lies about yourself. So, for example, someone at school may have said you were stupid, ugly or insignificant. Think about that. Where was the evidence? Was it just one person's opinion or a group of people's? Do you still believe it? Were you or are you guilty of something? Have you done something in the past that you're not proud of? What are you ashamed of? Are you ashamed of your past, or of your current job title? Do you wish you had a better up-bringing, more loving parents, more supportive teachers? Do you feel angry with yourself and the world? Write it all down. Let the raw truth about yourself come out.

Once you've written it all down, go through your list again and read it out loud. Once you've read it all, get out your pen and go to the first sentence. Cross it out. In fact, cross out every single thing you've written on your list, sentence by sentence. Yes, I want you to cross it *all* out.

Then, write this down, underneath that crossed out list:

'There are many things on this list I believe/believed about myself and there are also many things on this list that others used to label me. I know it's up to me, only, how I deal with these. I can choose to believe them or I can choose to let them go. I can continue to let other people's opinions control my life or I can let them go. I can choose to forgive myself for not treating myself the way I deserve to be treated, or I can continue living as I did. I know that I deserve love and acceptance from myself, and despite all my imperfections, I know that I am good enough, just as I am. I'm a unique person and I want to give myself the best life I possibly can. I want to enjoy this life adventure. I choose to love myself, even though some days I may find it harder to do than others. I'm willing to always choose love and acceptance. I'm ready to work on myself and start releasing that which no longer serves me. I'm ready to heal myself.'

This little exercise can help you see all the labels you've believed in the past, or may still be believing. This is the first step to your healing.

When speaking up is healing

One of my big fears is speaking up. It used to be a lot worse, but by facing my fear and putting myself 'out there', it got so much easier. Even though I've trained myself to be more confident, I still wander to this place more often than you'd think. Achieving a few credentials and being comfortable in front of a camera doesn't always mean you're not scared.

Picking up the phone and dealing with something that can't be resolved any other way or making a complaint at a department store, even when I'm in the right, can still sometimes be a little challenging for me. Why is that? I'm still afraid. I still haven't healed myself fully, released all my past fears and feelings of inadequacy. As everyone else, I'm still a work in progress and doing the best I can in any given moment. And sometimes that best is not what I'd like it to be. Many people who don't know me think I'm very confident. The truth is, my confidence is a learned skill. I don't mean I'm always faking it or that I'm pretending to be someone I'm not. What I do mean, however, is that we live in a tough world, and learning to be tough and becoming more confident is a necessity, especially for us introverts. On the other hand, I'm very confident in my ideas and beliefs, so this comes to me naturally. It's good to recognise our strengths and weaknesses because then we can start working towards improving ourselves. Naturally, I'm an introvert. I'm an introvert who has learned to sometimes express herself as an extrovert. In the past, I was very scared and shy and extremely uncomfortable talking to others. When the teacher asked questions at school, I was afraid to raise my hand, not because I didn't know the answer, but in case I was wrong. I was afraid of being laughed at, and rather than risk that happening I stayed quiet. Speaking up with confidence has always been a challenge for me, but it's also something I'm learning to master every day, and this has been incredibly healing. I'm amazed how much easier it got with daily practice and by having the willingness to keep working on myself.

Are you an introvert or afraid to speak up? Or perhaps you are both. You are not alone. For the next seven days I would like you to challenge yourself by doing the following exercise:

Step out of your comfort zone, take a deep breath and start speaking up in the situations where you normally wouldn't. This will feel new to you and it may feel somehow scary. Do it regardless of the discomfort you may be feeling. You owe it to yourself. Enough of missing opportunities. Enough to always stand in the background. Do you have something to say in a meeting? Say it. Do you feel like you have been treated unfairly by someone? Express how you feel.

I fully understand how vulnerable this may make you feel, but do yourself a big favour. Gather all the courage you have and do it anyway. I can promise you, you'll be so proud of yourself afterwards.

Learning to say *NO* – a big part of your healing process

Saying *No*, when we really mean *No*, can be very uncomfortable for some of us. Again, this has been one of my weaknesses, which I've been working on, and I'm pleased to say it's getting so much easier. Once we get into the habit of saying *No* when we really mean *No*, we can be unapologetic about it and say it with love and confidence. Saying *No* is truly an act of self-love and self-respect.

If someone asks you to do a favour for them, ask yourself these few simple questions:

How do I feel about it?

What is my intuition telling me?

Do I really want to do it?

Does this interfere with my own schedule?

Do I have time to do this?

Am I only saying Yes, so this person will continue to like me?

Do I really want to say Yes?

Am I saying Yes, so I don't upset this person?

When you say *No* to someone, you don't have to justify your response. You don't need to explain anything to anyone. Just be polite and assertive. Remember that *No* is also a complete sentence. If you feel like saying *Yes* to someone just to be nice, please don't. The other person will also feel it energetically. They'll know you are only saying *Yes* because you feel you have to say it. Don't be untruthful to yourself and others.

There may also be situations in life, where you're not sure straight away what to do and when you need to make your mind up about something later. If such a scenario occurs, don't be afraid to tell the other person you need to think about it and you will get back to them as soon as it's convenient. In this fast moving world, we often expect instant responses whether that's to text messages, emails or in person. This doesn't mean you too should become a mirror of the fast moving world. Take your time and think about what you really want to do, and what is important to you. Check your schedule and then get back to the person. Set your priorities. This is *your* life and only you should decide what you want to do with it. Nobody should be pressuring you to do something you don't want to do and you shouldn't let it happen. It can be hard to say *No*, because you don't like upsetting or disappointing people. I completely understand that. But you need, first of all, to be true to yourself and create your own boundaries so people don't take advantage of you. And on the other hand, when you *do* want to say *Yes*, say it with love and absolute certainty.

Setting boundaries

2010 was a year of big changes for me when my inner healing truly began. Little did I know at the time, that it would take years to shed many old energies and unlearn the bad habits which had caused me so much pain and anxiety. I'm still working on it, but the transformation I'm seeing is incredible. I'm learning to speak up more, and fear the world less. I'm learning to stand in my power and be the person I truly am without pretending or trying to impress anyone. It's not always an easy process, but I'm willing to be a life-long student, if I must. By sharing my stories with you, I want to help you become more authentic while you're working on improving yourself. I want to give you permission to step out of your comfort zone, so you can start becoming the person you truly are. I want to assist you in releasing the blocks that have been holding you back, so you can step into your truth fully. I want you to accept that it is okay to disappoint people when their requests don't resonate with your truth. And finally, I want you to know that you can let go of any old beliefs and labels others might have placed on you, and that you accepted.

Own your truth. Be who you came here to be. Don't be ashamed of your own story and show the world the beautiful person and soul that you truly are. Let your healing journey begin.

CHAPTER FIVE

TRANSFORMING

Last summer, on a sunny Saturday afternoon, my parents and I were sitting in the garden. We began talking about our good and not-so-good memories, and one of my memories from childhood came up. This made me very emotional and I burst into tears. I hadn't cried in front of my mum and dad for years. However, I wasn't embarrassed, but on the contrary, felt relieved and comforted, as I was surrounded by loved ones.

As I've mentioned earlier in the book, throughout my childhood and teenage years I was bullied, made fun of and laughed at. I'm not mentioning this to complain or seek attention so you'll feel sorry for me. I'm mentioning it because I want to help you turn your own struggles to your advantage. These early experiences create a platform for our life, from which everything else unfolds. And, when we believe in something very deeply, we begin seeing the evidence of it everywhere.

In the village I grew up in, they were several kids who picked on me daily. I kept asking myself, *Why me? What is wrong with me? Why do I have to go through this hardship? What have I done to deserve this? I've never done anything to anyone, I'm quiet, I'm minding my own business, why me?* I didn't know what the answer was. The bullies were attacking me and a few other kids who didn't know how to stand up for themselves, and it seemed like it was all happening for no reason. The bullies, however, would find a reason, such as wearing a jumper they didn't like, or having my hair loose instead of in a ponytail.

Later in life I realised that bullies, whether at school, at work or on social media are only insecure individuals who think they need to pick on others to be seen as powerful and tough. In truth, *they're* the weak ones. They have a low self-esteem, and they're unconsciously, showing their weakness by making fun of others. They're the ones who are searching for love, support and attention and may feel lost in life.

Looking back, I have a different outlook on these painful experiences. They might have been overwhelming at the time, but they've made me stronger as an adult. As a result of what happened, I became tougher and grew into a wise, independent and powerful woman. I learnt to stand up for myself and I learnt to speak up for myself. I learnt to be proud of who I am and put my needs first, even though some of the above took quite some time. I'm continually working on myself and generally, I'm doing quite well in life. I've achieved many incredible things and most importantly I've learnt to be me and love being me. Being bullied as a child toughened me up, so I became brave enough to start my own transformational journey to my truth.

Of course, when we re-visit painful past experiences, the pain may still be present and we may get emotional. This is only natural. But when we rise above such experiences and choose to view them from a higher perspective, a tremendous healing and transformation can take place in our lives. Suddenly we're not the victims anymore, instead, we're the survivors, the ones who have won.

This transformational journey I've set out on has been full of light and hope, but also full of dark and hopelessness. It has been filled with many exciting moments, but also with moments of anxiety and pain. Highs and lows are part of life, and we're always going to experience them whether we like it or not. As we've already learned, accepting the good and the bad as it comes is all part of the journey. The many challenges I've been through have been preparing me for something great, and I've also learnt, more than before, to appreciate and cherish the many moments of happiness and excitement. This will probably increase with age. As we get older we stop taking the everyday things for granted and realise they're not that ordinary, but rather, precious. I've found that by being grateful for what I have, for what's working and flowing in my life, right now, brings more things to be grateful for. It's in these moments that we're able to reach for some higher frequencies or energies and can become fully content in the moment.

Choosing to step out of the victim zone

Transformation doesn't always have to be difficult. You can flow through it with gratitude in your heart and peace in your soul. But transformation does require lots of courage and a choice to step out of the victim zone. What does it mean to be a victim? Put simply, a victim is a type of person which doesn't take responsibility for their own life and their own choices. They're choosing to stay in the victim zone and blame everyone else around them. The victim thinks they're always right and everyone else is wrong (however, this isn't to excuse anyone's poor behaviour towards you, that's their karma). A victim is a person who fears change and would rather suffer (if unintentionally) than take action to change something. However, someone who once was a victim can choose to step out of the victim zone and start taking responsibility for their life. I know this, because I used to be one. Taking responsibility for my own life has been one of the best choices I've ever made. When you do that, you've nobody else to blame. You stop blaming your teachers, your parents, your employer, the bullies, the government, the taxes, and so on, because you start seeing the big picture and that's life-transforming. When I did that, my life took a completely different direction and became more beautiful, because at that point I stopped wasting my energy on unimportant things and I started focusing on me and what truly mattered in my life. Of course, it's not an easy process, setbacks happen, you get angry, you feel irritated or you become frustrated.

Make a decision

So how do you begin? By deciding. Decide right now, that you're not going to be a victim anymore. This often happens when you've just had enough and you get very fed up with everything. You reach the point where being a victim is no longer an option. This stage is a huge blessing because it opens many new doors you haven't been able to see before.

Our entire life is about choice. You're choosing to turn up to the job you don't like, you're choosing to stay in a relationship which doesn't work anymore, you're choosing to stay overweight, you're choosing to remain where you are. It's all your choice. When you start to understand this, a shift can occur in your life.

You may disagree with me and say that you've a mortgage to pay, and you have to eat, and so on, and that's why you go to the job you don't want to go to. But, actually, you choose to go because you've accepted commitments such as paying that mortgage, and also because you're a responsible person. But again, ask yourself, whether taking responsibility is continuously complaining about your job *or* taking action to start creating something better on the side, while you're still working there. I'd choose the latter.

I'm not saying this so you can feel bad or judge yourself. Just think about it. You're learning about transformation and I'm simply presenting you with a different perspective. This book hasn't been written to make you feel bad, but rather to teach you how to love and accept yourself for who you are, and make you more powerful in your truth. The book has also been designed to share some new ideas, ones you maybe haven't thought about before, so you can start creating something better for yourself, something that will make your existence happier and more meaningful, even though you may still feel lost or live in fear.

So if, like me, you were bullied as a child, or believe you're unworthy or insignificant, ask yourself whether you still want to believe this. Make a choice, once and for all, that you're not going to choose this story anymore and you're not going to be a victim. Create a different story by making different choices. What you focus on always expands. When you choose to believe in something, the Universe will be presenting you with confirmations of this. That's how powerful you truly are. Everything has a frequency. In order to create a transformation in your life, you need to change your frequency. So, start seeing yourself in a different light. Choose to see yourself as someone who is powerful and capable of amazing things. Start looking at yourself as a creator of your physical reality. Start looking at yourself as someone who is more than ready to change your life for the better and create your own opportunities, just by changing your perspective. You're the master of your life. No-one is in charge, only you. You're in charge of your own transformation and you can make it as fun and as beautiful a process as you want. It's all up to you, because *you're* in control. You're not a victim, unless you choose to be a victim. Life is too short to play small, or to be a victim. Make a firm choice to become a conscious creator of your own reality and you'll start seeing the world you've been desiring for a long time.

Breaking old patterns and letting go of limiting beliefs

I used to have a problem with my body image. Even though I knew I was a pretty girl, I didn't love myself. I was always finding faults, whether it was with my hair, my nose being too big, my teeth not being straight enough, or not being at my ideal weight. I was critical of myself and very insecure. And, as we know, when you're convinced about something (even if it isn't true, or that bad), the world often reflects it back to you. In some of my past relationships, my boyfriends at the time would frequently point out all that was wrong with me, and that's because I secretly felt that way myself. Life is like a mirror. We will delve deeper into this in the next chapter.

One of my issues was food. Over a decade ago, when I was changing many of my old life patterns, I was also changing my relationship with food. I'd never had a good relationship with food. I was either an overeater or I'd eat very little. I'd either put on weight or be under weight. At one point, my weight got so low, it began to be serious. I had to learn how to eat mindfully, as well as unlearn some bad habits that weren't serving me well and were putting my health at risk. At that point, I was upset with myself, my ways of living and I was angry with the whole world. Since then, I've managed to let go of many of my worst eating habits, although some issues still come back, seasonally. The good news is that I don't resent myself for it anymore. I know we're all a work-in-progress and are doing the best we can, at any given moment. We can still get off-track. That's what being a human being means.

I choose to love myself while doing my best every day. It isn't always easy, but I've found that loving myself, despite what's going on, has allowed me to feel more at peace with myself and my imperfections, as well as with the world around me.

Self-care – an important key to your transformation

You *are* important and you *are* worthy, because you exist. You deserve the same amount of love, support and care that you give to others. We often forget to look after ourselves because we're too busy living lives and doing things. Your self-care should be your number one priority. You need to nourish yourself and look after yourself every day, the best way you can. When you do that, you'll start feeling more energised and it will make you happier too. I know that life can be very hectic sometimes and you may feel that you don't have time for anything. We all have things that occupy our time such as going to work, meeting deadlines, looking after children and so on. We may be aware of feeling tired but we rarely acknowledge this and often only do so when something goes wrong, such as when we get ill. It's at this point that we finally realise that we can't carry on like this anymore.

Slowing down

One day, while rushing around London, I realised something profound which changed my outlook on life forever. I often see spiritual signs around me, but that day they were screaming out loud. *Slowing down* was the theme that day. Traffic lights turned red while I was driving, there were queues at every shop I went to, and the internet connection wasn't working properly when I tried to send a quick email. It was overwhelming and my over-controlling attitude was making it even worse. At that point, I couldn't ignore the universe's messages I was being presented with. I needed to slow down, then stop and acknowledge what was going on. I decided to take a few deep breaths and this calmed me down. I decided then to focus on what I was dealing with in the current moment, instead of on several things at the same time, or even thinking about what to do next. Focusing on one thing at a time not only created better results, but it also kept my attention in the present moment. When I got home, I made myself a lovely dinner, and had a nice long bath which relaxed me. Afterwards, I lit some candles and rested on the sofa. Doing all this made a huge difference to how I'd felt just a few hours ago. Since then, I try not to rush around so much any-more. I can be quick doing things, but I've learned how to be quick, but be calm too. I look after myself more. My self-care is my priority.

Planning your self-care day

Slowing down and taking some time off, just for yourself, isn't a waste of time. You'll actually gain more time. You'll become more rested and energised, and you'll be surprised how much you'll be able to accomplish later. I now schedule my self-care days and put them into my diary. Self-care days are an important part of my schedule. You too can plan a self-care day, put it in your diary and make it non-negotiable. This is *your* time and you can do whatever pleases you. Remember, this isn't a waste of time, it's an act of self-love and shows respect for yourself. Do this often and you'll see what a difference it makes to your life and the transformation that comes with it. I also understand this could be quite difficult when you have small children. If you do, taking an hour or just a few minutes for yourself, from time to time, can be quite therapeutic.

Be kinder to yourself

As humans we can be very self-critical and judge ourselves harshly. Many of us think we're not good enough and we don't do enough, we compare ourselves with others and think we should be somewhere we're currently not. We believe that when we gain certain credentials, certain possessions or get into a relationship, *then* we'll be happy. Thinking this way means not only are we postponing our true happiness and living in the future, but puts us at risk of becoming edgy, uneasy and often exhausted. We're not kind to ourselves, instead we're hard on ourselves. Again, I speak for myself here.

I'm a perfectionist. I like to have things done in a certain way and I often have high expectations of myself. This isn't necessarily a bad thing, because I've also learned some valuable lessons through my perfectionism. But now I know when I go overboard with this and need to take a step back. I've learned to accept that it's okay not to be perfect. I've learned to pause and breathe and focus on what really matters in life. I've learned to be kinder to myself. How do you become kinder to yourself? Here are a few tips:

Begin by praising yourself instead of being critical. Tell yourself how well you're doing. For example, look in the mirror and say to yourself: *'I'm so proud of you. You have done so well today!'* If something doesn't work out the way you hoped it would, be kind to yourself and say: *'You've done your very best today and you've learned some new lessons. Next time, you'll do so much better. You can do it. Don't give up!'* Encouraging yourself every day is essential. I praise and encourage myself on a daily basis. It empowers me. You are allowed to make mistakes in life, so don't be afraid to make them. That's how you learn. Stop being so judgemental towards yourself and be kinder.

Another way in which you can be kinder to yourself is to accept compliments from others. Many people don't know how to accept compliments. If someone says they love your hair or that you've done a great job at something, don't reject it by saying: *'Don't be silly,'* etc. Simply say, *'Thank you!'* That's it. I used to have problems in this area, but now I accept compliments with gratitude. It's an act of unconditional love towards myself which I truly deserve. Accepting compliments will not only increase your self-esteem, but it will also teach you to love and appreciate yourself more. It's another step on your transformational journey.

And lastly, become kinder to yourself by listening to your body and your soul. Pay attention to the messages your body and soul are giving you. When you feel tired, take a break. When you feel you need a holiday, organise it. It doesn't have to be far away or expensive. It can be a weekend getaway to the mountains or a camping trip. If you lack energy, think about what you're eating, talk to a nutritionist and/or make dietary adjustments. Exercise. Any kind of exercise is good. You don't have to go to the gym, if it doesn't resonate with you. You can always exercise at home even if it's only for ten minutes. Ten minutes is better than no exercise at all. You can go for a walk in nature. I don't go to the gym, but I take ballet classes, do yoga and exercise at home. You make the rules. Listen to your body when it's telling you to sleep. Try having a good night's sleep as often as possible. Look after yourself and listen to your body and your soul. They're always talking to you. Let their voice overtake your mind's voice, which is often louder and not always what you need to hear.

Begin your transformational journey today. Practise the suggested exercises in this chapter and start experiencing the results you've been longing for, and which you truly deserve.

CHAPTER SIX

CREATING

What you're seeing in your life right now is the result of the choices you've made up to this point. We briefly touched on this in Chapter Five. The beliefs you've accepted deeply and the things others have said about you that you've never questioned, all of these have in some form shaped your outer experiences. What you focus on always expands and the evidence of that expansion easily presents itself in the physical world as a *by-product*. You start to perceive and experience the things you believe in. You may have beliefs which are serving you well, and some which aren't. Some of your beliefs may be making your life difficult, they may even be harmful to you. They may be keeping you stuck in a vicious circle, or in the past. You may be a person with much potential, great qualities and many talents, but the beliefs you're holding could be doing you a disservice.

The good news is that you're the creator of your own reality. Yes, you are. You always have a choice about what you want to believe in and what you don't want to believe. You can make a decision right now that you're no longer going to believe all the lies which have been harmful to you and are currently holding you back. You can make a decision that you're going to start creating a fresh new reality for yourself, and you're soon going to see the evidence of it. Then that evidence has no other choice but to start appearing around you. It may take a little while, but with a daily reminder that you're not a victim of your current circumstances, but rather a creator of them, you're going to start experiencing some great results.

In my life I've wrestled with many negative beliefs which were deeply buried within my subconscious, so much so that I wouldn't even class them as beliefs, but as facts. I was seeing the evidence of these beliefs on a daily basis and I hated it. People in my life, whether close to me, or random strangers were reflecting these beliefs back to me. The beliefs were screaming at me from every corner. What we believe about ourselves is always reflected back to us. Sometimes, some of my deepest fears, which I still believed but pretended I didn't, were thrown into my face by other people's behaviour. The behaviour annoyed me but it was only a reflection of my own wounded self and the things I didn't want to see. The people were sent to me as a reminder that I still had work to do and lots of inner healing to get through. Instead of judging them, I was given the opportunity to go even deeper within myself and find the root of the problem I needed to deal with, rather than ignoring it and pretending I had it all together.

When we create what we don't want to

Alan is a young man in his late twenties. He's quiet, shy, insecure and often keeps his emotions to himself. Recently, he started a new job at a printing company. All was going well, except for one thing. One of his work colleagues was making unnecessary comments and this was making Alan feel very uncomfortable. He felt the man didn't like him and was deliberately causing trouble. Being new to the company, Alan kept quiet about it and suffered in silence. Two months later, the colleague was still being annoying towards him. When Sunday evening arrived, the thought of seeing the man on Monday made Alan feel stressed and anxious. Alan worked hard to get the job and enjoys it, but because of this one person he'd stopped looking forward to going to work.

When Monday arrived he got upset again because of the man's comments, but this time he decided to talk to one of his colleagues about it. She told him to ignore this man, as he had a reputation for picking on others. He had a strange attitude and, she explained, in most companies you find at least one person like that. Alan felt a bit better after talking to his colleague, but he still didn't understand how someone could behave like this when he didn't even know him.

Alan's example is a clear example of life being a mirror. He's shy, worried and a bit insecure. His insecurities, which he doesn't talk about, and is hiding, are thrown in his face when he encounters an unpleasant work colleague who picks on him. Alan is unintentionally bringing up to the surface what he doesn't want others to see, and it's manifesting right in front of him. He's creating what he doesn't want because of the beliefs in his subconscious. Alan needs to learn to stand in his power and ask himself: *'What do I have to learn from this situation? What is it in me that I need to heal and release, so I can stop attracting people who are pointing out my insecurities? How can I become more confident and yet still stay true to myself?'*

We create our own reality by our thoughts, emotions and beliefs. Our own insecurities are often reflected in the physical reality, no matter how hard we try to hide them. Look at such situations as an opportunity for growth, a chance to look inward and start transforming what's making our life difficult. Stop being angry at the world, because what we experience is only a reflection of our wounded self and an opportunity for a deeper healing and transformation.

Doing one thing a day that scares you

We all have our own insecurities. These insecurities are burdens which make our lives unnecessarily difficult. I find that by doing at least one thing a day that scares you, you can grow in confidence and increase your self-esteem. It doesn't have to be anything big. I'm not suggesting jumping out of an aeroplane or going abseiling. It can be something small. As I've already said, I used to be afraid of making phone calls. This was partly because of my accent and because I was afraid people wouldn't understand me, but also because I was scared to speak up and express what I wanted in life. These two factors made picking up the phone a scary experience. Once I realised that I was missing out on opportunities and not speaking up when something wasn't right and needed addressing, I made a decision not to be 'silly' anymore and to pick up the phone without hesitation. I forced myself to make phone calls, despite my fear. After a while, I decided to take it further and face my other insecurities. The results were astonishing. This has not only made me more confident and increased my self-esteem, it has also helped me stop attracting people into my life who'd challenge me or point out these in-securities. Try this exercise for at least a couple of weeks and see how much confidence you'll gain.

What does living a creative life mean to you?

It was always my creativity that helped me to keep myself above water. No matter how bad I felt, no matter what I was going through, my creativity was my saviour. It nourished my soul and it helped me get onto a pos-itive frequency when I felt down. You're the creator of your own reality, as you've just learned, but you should also be *expressing yourself creatively in life*, whatever this means to you.

If you go back to the introduction of this book, you'll remember that I'm describing a painful experience, standing in front of the mirror in my hotel room in Hong Kong. That day, I felt awful. I realised how broken I still was and I questioned myself, my work and the point of everything I was doing in life. After almost an hour of feeling hopeless and powerless, an idea struck me. I was guided to share my feelings by writing a very honest book. It is this book that you're reading right now. The idea for the book came out of that hopeless moment, which started dissolving the moment I turned my computer on, and decided to write the first sentence. Even though I felt powerless at the time, I was magically re-directed back to my purpose. By being in physical and emotional pain, I remembered that this was an opportunity to talk to others about my feelings and perhaps to inspire them to start facing their own struggles, to stop being afraid and to give others hope. My creativity, once again, led me back to my purpose in life.

Doing what you love

What do you love doing? What do you do by choice? All of us came to the earth with so many amazing gifts which are unique and valuable. There has never been anybody like you and there is never going to be. Therefore, it's important to awaken your creative genius that possesses all these amazing gifts. Your dreams matter and your creativity is an internal compass leading you to your beautiful and *one in a lifetime purpose* on this planet. We all have a purpose here and that purpose is unique to every single one of us.

Our souls long to express themselves in creative ways because this is the way we bring joy to ourselves and bring joy to others too. You are an amazing creator that came to the earth to leave an imprint of your uniqueness, no matter how big or small. You came here to express yourself creatively and leave a mark for others to get inspired by. There is a magic within you, waiting to be discovered and shared with the world.

Start creating something today. Choose whatever comes to mind. It doesn't have to be anything big. Get creative by baking a beautiful cake, get creative in your garden or re-organise your bookshelf. Do it for yourself, for your own healing. Once you've started, be proud of every step you take and enjoy the process. Have fun.

If you decide to do something bigger than being creative in the kitchen, keep going and don't give up. It may be a longer process than baking a cake, but know that it's not about the final product, but about the journey. Carry on, no matter what, even when you have to take a break for a few days or weeks. When you feel inspiration has left you, look around you. Inspiration lies in every corner of this earth and beyond. It's just a matter of noticing it and tuning into it. Notice the magic the universe has in store for you. There's so much in your favour. Continue creating what only you, with your own unique perspective can create.

Let go of worrying about what other people think of you. That really has nothing to do with you. Keep believing in yourself and if it brings you happiness, keep doing it.

Some of you may think you may be too old to begin something new. If so, you're mistaken. You're never too old to start anything. Do it, even if it's only for fun. When I was training to be a pilot, we had a gentleman at the flying school who started taking flying lessons at the age of seventy-two. He'd never flown before, but was ready for a new challenge, a new adventure that would take him to new heights in life. He believed in himself and did it for the fun of it. What an inspiration. I also know of many dancers, yoga teachers and actors who started taking classes well over the age of 50. That's what living creatively truly means. Being creative is a beautiful way of aligning with your authentic self while you're wandering through life. Our creativity comes from our souls, it's a form of all the beautiful intuitive whispers, which become ideas and then creations. Listen to these whispers, don't doubt them and you'll be led towards something that may even surprise you.

Bringing dreams into reality the creative way

The older I get, the more I'm noticing how edgy and uncomfortable procrastinating in relation to my dreams makes me feel. Time is passing, and every day that ends isn't coming back. I don't want this to sound depressing or negative but, *what are we all waiting for? Why are we postponing and putting on hold all these beautiful dreams we have?'*

This is what often happens to people when they set upon living a creative life. They encounter an obstacle, and then they suddenly don't know what to do, wondering which way they should turn. Many, unfortunately doubt themselves to the extent that they eventually stop. The beautiful idea they were so excited about just about a week or a month ago starts fading away.

Why do we put off things we really want to do, often pushing them aside, and waiting for a better time? That better time may never come. Our dreams should be our priority. Even one small step today is a step, and forward is always forward. You don't want to regret things later, just because you didn't feel like doing it today. We need to act and enjoy this journey while we can. Don't put off until tomorrow what you can do today. That class you always wanted to take, the phone call that could change your life, the book you always wanted to write: these are just some examples. Start today, even if only for ten minutes. We all come up with excuses why we can't follow our dream, why it's not possible. But remember, you're the one who creates. You're making the decision. Instead, think of at least three reasons every day why you can do this. Create deadlines. There are seven days in the week and *someday* isn't one of them. Creating deadlines can be a great way to get things done. I do this all the time. I pencil a date and time for my creative work in my diary. When it's written down, I know I will get on with it and get the work done no matter how many excuses my mind comes up with. I make it non-negotiable. Start today, not on Monday, or next month. I often see how many beautiful dreams don't get fulfilled, because of procrastination or a fear of failure. Let me give you an example:

I met a girl once who wanted to become a private pilot. When I was telling her how I became a private pilot myself and how exciting the journey was, even though it was hard at times, I could see the sparkle in her eyes and her eagerness to take up the challenge. She said she would book a flying lesson the following week. Several years later, unfortunately, she hasn't booked her trial flying lesson. She got excited about it for a day or two, maybe longer, and then she let it go. When a dream is born, most people get excited. Maybe for a few days, a week, or a month or so. Later, when they realise how much work they'll have to put into accomplishing it, most take a step back and some never begin. But it doesn't have to be that way.

I find that breaking the process down and looking at it as a creative challenge is the way to go. By being disciplined enough and taking small steps every day, and by not giving up, we can bring our dreams into reality. They landed in our consciousness, because we were the right people to bring them into the world. When we do so, we'll not only achieve something great, but we'll also inspire others to start their own creative process. In her bestseller *The 5 Second Rule*, author and motivational speaker, *Mel Robbins*, suggests taking 5 second decisions to overcome procrastination. By counting down from 5 to 1, and taking action within that 5-second window, we can stop procrastination. I've been using *The 5 Second Rule* for quite some time now and I highly recommend reading Mel's book. It's absolutely incredible and full of wonderful suggestions. So, what's preventing you from starting something great today? Don't postpone your creative ideas. Whatever your idea is, take the first step today and become one of the few who make their dreams come true.

Overcoming procrastination

I have a three-step formula which can help you overcome procrastination, if you're willing to put in some work:

1) Begin now

If you really want to make something happen and it's important to you, you will find a way, if not, you'll find an excuse why you can't do it. What can you do today that will get you closer to your dream? Is it reading a book? Read a page. Is it signing up for a class? Book it. Is it sending that email? Send it today.

2) Stop talking, start doing

Many people talk about their dreams, but that's about it. They get inspired and excited about their new ideas for a while, but never take any action. They always have some kind of excuse why they can't do it yet. What a waste of their precious time on earth. Don't be one of those people. Stop talking and start taking action today. Don't even mention it to anyone. Most people who have big dreams, often don't tell a soul but quietly work towards their goal. No one needs to know. Everyone can find out later what you've been up to.

3) Enjoy it

Following your dreams should be a fun process. Even though you should be taking daily action, which may be hard at times, don't let it become a chore, something you dread and do because you have to. Have fun along the way and enjoy it. Don't be too serious about it, otherwise, you'll get fed up and demotivated. Make the process enjoyable. Let me give you an example: I write a lot. Writing is my art and it brings so much happiness to my soul. But to make my writing even more enjoyable, I made a little ritual for it too. I always make myself a cup of tea. When I'm writing from home, I open the windows, so I can hear the birds, and I put gentle music on, or I listen to a recording of rain or a thunderstorm as background music, which helps my creativity. I also light a candle and create a peaceful setting for my writing. It works like magic.

Create an art you'll be proud of

Living a creative life is an art, and you're the artist. You're the one who's creating your own story. Your art is the product of that story. Start painting a picture of what you want to see, by adding the colours you like, so you can make that picture something to be proud of, and also something that inspires others. Follow your heart, rise above your insecurities, keep creating, never give up and most importantly, enjoy it.

CHAPTER SEVEN

ADVENTURING

I sometimes have a deep fear of how life is going to unfold for me. Even though I teach and coach people and I can have good ideas which can help shift others' perspectives, I'm still human and have my own fears and worries. When it comes to my own life, I sometimes worry a lot. I worry what's going to happen next, I worry about my family's health, about my boyfriend, my career and my finances. I sometimes create all sorts of frightening scenarios in my mind which make me feel down and scared. Being in my thirties, at the time of writing this, I often ask, where did my twenties go? Watching my sister's children grow up so quickly, I'm seeing how quickly time flies. Sometimes I wonder where I'd be, if I took a different path in life? Then I become upset that I haven't accomplished as much as others my age. Where is fame, recognition and fulfilment? Sometimes, I'm led to thinking about being an old lady, and asking myself how well I lived my life? Where am I going with this?

All of us have similar thoughts or fears, occasionally, but most of us don't talk about them. Asking these kinds of questions and wondering about the answers can bring up fear and nostalgia, so we push it away and don't talk about it. But lately, I've discovered something incredible. I find that when I actually express my deep fears and concerns to others, I no longer feel alone and these concerns don't seem so scary anymore. They no longer prey on my mind as much. When my mind wanders to such places now, I talk to my boyfriend and he comforts me and reminds me that I'm not alone. I also find that sharing what I'm going through, through my weekly articles, brings comfort and peace to my soul. In such instances, people often share their own experiences with me and this way we support each other, no matter where we are in life. I don't want to be one of those coaches or teachers who pretends they have all the answers and everything in their life is perfect. Nobody's life is perfect. Being honest with people creates more genuine connections and soulful conversations.

The truth about fear

Even though being afraid is unpleasant and annoying, fear can be a wonderful teacher. Fear can be extremely overwhelming and it's an emotion that keeps us stuck where we don't want to be, but fear itself doesn't need to be scary. It comes from the mind and anything created by our mind can be transformed and seen from a different perspective, if we choose to see it that way. I'm not here to teach you how to overcome fear, because I'm still fearful of so many things in life. But what I'm going to show you, is how to cooperate with fear. Fear is part of our life's adventure, so we need to start accepting it and stop pushing it away.

When I was learning to fly, I was excited about flying but I was also scared. At the time, I didn't really talk about my fear, even though some of my flying instructors could probably sense it. The most important thing was that I wanted to learn to fly. I absolutely loved flying. I was determined to study and do the work. At the same time, I was scared. But no matter how uncomfortable I felt back then, I had one advantage. I always looked fear straight into the face and did what I had to do anyway. I'm not sure where this courage came from, but it always served me amazingly well. This doesn't mean I never hesitated. I did, and I still do, in so many areas of my life, but it didn't matter how long it took me, in the end I faced my fear. I realised that the only way to overcome fear was to cooperate with it. It is the cooperation that has helped me accomplish some great things in life and that's the reason why I want to talk to you about it.

We're all scared, but some of us hide our fears better than others. I can certainly raise both hands for this one. But I've also found that admitting we're scared and accepting the bodily sensations that fear brings with it, can be extremely liberating. That's how we cooperate with fear. It can make you feel vulnerable, but there's strength in your vulnerability. Why pretend to ourselves we're not scared, when we're frightened? This is extremely damaging to our body, mind and soul. Being afraid is part of life, whether we like it or not. Admitting this to yourself, accepting your feelings and cooperating with them is, in my opinion, a sign of great strength. There's absolutely no shame admitting that you are in fear.

As I keep wandering through life, more and more fear still comes up

A few years ago, I attended a 'Fear of Public Speaking' course. I was excited about it, but at the same time, I was scared. I knew, when you attend these sorts of courses you can't just sit there, listen and take notes. You have to stand up and do a presentation or several, in front of a group of complete strangers. The thought made me very uncomfortable, but I signed up for the course anyway. My goal was to become a more confident speaker and I was willing to do what was needed to make it happen. I wanted my voice to be heard. I had plans to teach more and speak more in public, so not attending the course wasn't an option. You know that feeling when you feel you want to be doing something, but you're still scared to do it? That's how I felt.

So, despite my fear, I turned up for my training. My teacher, Vince, made me feel very comfortable straight away. He welcomed me with a warm smile and a firm handshake. I was one of the first people in the classroom that morning and I sat down in the front row while we all waited for the other students to arrive. My palms began to sweat. I had butterflies in my stomach and my throat was getting tighter and tighter. Then, while we were still waiting, my teacher approached me and started asking me some general questions. He put me at my ease again and I calmed down. I'd acknowledged, after all, that I was at the 'Fear of Public Speaking' course and everybody there was in a similar position. We were all afraid of speaking in public and that was why we were there. I decided to stop thinking about it so much and focus on one thing at a time. I'd do what I was asked to do, and try to enjoy the course, despite my discomfort.

Then, the time came when I had to stand in front of the group and give my first five-minute presentation. My palms began to sweat again and it felt like I had a lump in my throat. I was worried my fellow students wouldn't understand my accent and I had all sorts of other excuses on my mind. Then, I surprised myself. I spoke clearly and naturally, making eye contact with my audience and teacher, even though I was feeling very nervous and uncomfortable. I delivered my lines successfully and everyone clapped. It became easier with each presentation I had to deliver. I was glad I'd made the decision to sign up for the course, despite my fear. In the end, I completed the course successfully. The course proved to me, once again, that the only way to overcome something, or at least become more comfortable with it, was to face it and cooperate with it.

If you don't try you'll never know. Whether it was my pilot training, the public speaking course or some challenging situation, taking it step by step, one day at the time, and accepting the feeling I was feeling, helped me to become more and more comfortable. I can't say I'm feeling one hundred percent confident when I speak in public now, I don't. But I now know that the only way to speak in public, which I love doing despite my fear, is to just go for it. Why would you stop yourself doing something you feel you need to do? Why would you continue wondering what if? Take a leap of faith, despite your fear and do it. You might surprise yourself.

Yes, you can

So what is it you're afraid to do? What is it that you think about all the time and know that if you finally did it, you'd feel free? And what can you do today to bring yourself a step closer to it? Get your special notebook out and write your answers down. When you finish writing, I'd like you to close your eyes and visualise the following:

Visualise a person who's already doing something you want to accomplish. Is it a celebrity? A famous athlete? An author? Or someone you know of who is very confident? Ask them for advice. Ask them how they would deal with the fear you have? Ask them any question you have on your mind and listen for the answer. They may have some great insights for you.

Then, visualise the following:

You've faced your fear and you are now doing what you were dreaming about. How do you feel? What sort of emotions are you experiencing? Go into detail. Are there people congratulating you on your achievement? What can you see, hear, touch, taste and smell? Yes, apply *all* your senses to this vision. That's how dreams become reality. You have to feel these feelings *Now*. Say to yourself, that you're so happy and grateful that you've finally done it. Tell yourself how proud of yourself you are. Feel the feelings of happiness and accomplishment now.

Remember, that in your mind, you can go anywhere and do anything.

This is a very powerful exercise and I highly recommend you do it daily. It can only take five minutes of your day, but it can create life-changing benefits in your life.

Be the courageous one

I still face many challenges, but I'm moving forward, daily, because I know that's the only way to enjoy my adventure fully. I know I can do this, and so can you. You were given this life because you're strong enough to live it. All these challenges, all these struggles, but also the dreams you have, are teaching you some amazing lessons, which are going to be revealed to you later. They're making you stronger and wiser. Please promise me that you won't give up. Always keep going. And if you get off the track, don't worry, take a deep breath and try again. Say yes to new adventures, even though they may seem scary and uncomfortable sometimes. Say yes to them, not because you want to prove something to someone else, but because you want to do it for yourself. Let others live their own lives and worry about their own adventure. Your adventure is yours and yours alone. Prove to yourself only, that you're more than capable of embracing whatever you choose. And what can you do for others? Instead of trying to be a show off, inspire them by living your truth and being the best version of yourself you can be. Stay raw and real, scared and unsure, messy and uncomfortable, but striving to do your best anyway.

Life can be scary because you don't know where you're going and where you may end up. Life can be uncomfortable, because you're constantly facing the unknown. At the same time, life is incredible. Be courageous and set out on an unknown path to try something new, something great. It takes courage to step out of your comfort zone. It takes courage to face your fears, but what's the point of this journey otherwise? To stay at home and sit on the sofa with a cup of tea? No. To be courageous means to live. Take a step forward today and see where it leads.

CHAPTER EIGHT

LEARNING

A while ago, my boyfriend told me he'd met one of his regular customers who asked him how he was doing. He replied: *'Great! I've just come back from a lovely holiday with my girlfriend and her family.'* His customer said: *'Are you still with her?'* My boyfriend replied: *'Of course.'* The man said: *'Never trust an Eastern European. All they want is your money.'* My boyfriend, shocked, said: *'Well, that's what you think, but you don't know my girlfriend and who she is. She's an amazing person who always helps others, never uses anyone, and is a giver. She's an educated, accomplished young woman. One of the most generous and nicest people I've ever known.'* The man then said that none of that meant anything, because I was from Eastern Europe. William, my boyfriend, was very disappointed because he'd known this man for some time and wouldn't have expected him to say anything like that. It made him change his mind about him. The man's wife, who was also there, looked embarrassed and shocked.

When I heard what this man had said, I was upset. This man had never even met me, but unfortunately, his opinions had prompted him to say these hurtful things, which made him look silly. Just because I was born in Slovakia doesn't mean I can't be trusted or would take advantage of anyone. It made me wonder how people came up with these kinds of ideas. Why do people judge others based on their nationality, religion or skin colour? I was born in Slovakia. Does this mean I should be put into a certain category? Or, if someone happens to be born in a so-called, well-developed country, does that make them better than others? It doesn't make sense. People often don't realise how their unwise comments can crush someone's confidence and make them feel small, especially people who already have low self-esteem and not much confidence. The man's unpleasant comment upset me, but I didn't believe what he said, so I got over it quite quickly. My boyfriend wasn't sure whether to tell me, at first, but because we're both honest with each other, he decided he would. I'm pleased he did because I always learn so much from these examples and then I can help other people through similar situations.

Your nationality, religion, skin colour, job title, or whatever label the world gives you doesn't define you. Because, for example, you were born in a part of the world that isn't considered a great empire, or something amazing, doesn't mean that you're less than anybody else. Such ideas are illusions. Who came up with them in the first place? We need to let go of these nonsensical lies once and for all and start creating a world that is happy and comfortable *for everyone*. The planet belongs to *all of us*, despite where we're from, and we should all have the opportunity to experience it fully.

Yes, it makes me frustrated and fearful to write about this. But at the same time, it also makes me feel strong about my opinions and the truth I'm ready to fully step into and share with you. The world needs to wake up. We need to treat every person as an individual, as a fellow human being, an occupant of this earth and a citizen of the universe. That's who we really are. Let's look beyond the labels and the lies and rise above them. Let's start looking at such opinions as outdated ideas from the past, and too pathetic to even talk about. Let's be more kind to each other. Let's make our experience on the earth happy and fulfilling, each of us working to raise the consciousness of this planet and the entire universe.

But what can we do today to create more unity rather than living in separation? Is there something we can do to become wiser, and live at peace with each other, rather than believing the lies and illusions? How can we educate the unaware people, like the man who put me into a category and made unpleasant comments, before he'd even met me? There are few things we can do.

Be an example

Becoming an example to others and living our truth can be a huge step. We don't have to preach anything to anyone, but by simply being kind and compassionate towards others, we can inspire others to do the same. I believe this is a better choice than being pushy and loud. We can't get far by demand, but being a living example of what we believe in, and what we care about, we can help wake up those who are asleep.

If your journey is a difficult one, you've been given an opportunity

If you've been born in a country that's not considered important, or of interest to others, you've been given a great opportunity to use this to your advantage. You have the opportunity to rise above the label you've been given, and show others how proud you are of the place you were born. Show the world that people from this country are equal to everyone else. Don't be ashamed of your background or your story – prove the lies wrong. Educate others and let them know (but not in a pushy way) that you deserve the same respect as everyone else and shouldn't be looked down on. You have the same right to exist as others and you're worthy because you were born. If you feel unworthy or less than worthy, put this out of your mind right now. I know it can be difficult, especially if you're a *foreigner* living in another country. I've been facing this my whole adult life and it's not always easy. We meet all sorts of people and not all of them are welcoming. But remember, you're the citizen of this world, a citizen of the universe, and you have the same right to exist as everyone else. You can promote this truth and let others know that it's finally time to look beyond the old-fashioned labels. I've used the example here, of being from a foreign country, but this philosophy works with any label you've been given. There's a beautiful quote by Nelson Mandela that speaks for itself: *'No one is born hating another person because of the colour of his skin, or his background, or his religion. People must learn to hate, and if they can learn to hate, they can be taught to love, for love comes more naturally to the human heart than its opposite.'*

You are enough

You are as good as anybody else. No one should be putting you down and make you feel inferior. You're also powerful enough to embrace and rise above any challenges you face. So, if you've ever felt unworthy or experienced nasty or unfair comments from people, like the one I described earlier, please know you're not alone. At the same time, please know that if the person who made the negative comment was a happy, grounded and loving person, they wouldn't have said it. They would have kept any such thoughts to themselves, and maybe one day felt embarrassed, suddenly seeing that they needed to wake up and educate themselves. Look at this as an invitation to your greatness. Look at it as a new opportunity to hold your head high, to become stronger and be there for others who may be facing something similar.

Self-worth

I opened the chapter with this example because I wanted to point out how much, collectively and as individuals, we still have to learn. Educating each other properly is a major step in living more peaceful and fulfilling lives. That's what we're all longing for. But unfortunately, the separation here on this planet is preventing us from feeling that peace and experiencing that fulfilment.

How can we begin the true learning, the true education? Begin with the steps above: by being an example, seeing the opportunity in your 'disadvantage' and knowing that after all, you are enough.

What we need to do next is increase our self-worth. In Chapter Five we talked about self-care. Self-worth is a one step up from self-care. I believe that when you increase your self-worth, you will gain confidence which will radiate from you naturally. When confidence radiates from you, others will pick up on it too and they will treat you the way you deserve to be treated. Of course, you can't always prevent comments, similar to my boyfriend's former customer, but by knowing your self-worth, you'll be able to stand in your power fully, because you know who you are and the petty comments won't matter as such. Even though such a comment may upset you for a while, like it upset me, you'll be able to rise above the ignorance and immaturity of the critic quickly, because at that point you'll know that there's no point in giving it too much time and energy.

Exercise

Get your notebook out again because I have a great exercise for you. On the top of the page write down: *I am an amazing woman/man because:*

Then, start listing all the amazing things about yourself. This exercise is designed to increase your self-worth.

Here is my example:

'I am an amazing woman, because I care deeply about others. I have a good heart and I am genuine. I am an amazing woman, because I follow my dreams every single day and by doing so, I know I can help others. I am an amazing woman because I take care of myself. I know that when I am well and taken care of, then I can be of great service to the world. When I'm fulfilled and overflowing with joy, then I can share this with others. I am an amazing woman, because I'm a giver. I love giving to others and I know they appreciate it.'

The list can be as long as you like. You can write pages and pages of it, praising yourself, listing all your accomplishments and the things about yourself that you're proud of. This beautiful exercise helped me to appreciate myself more. It helped raise my confidence, and I'd been lacking confidence for a long time. Give the exercise a try and start increasing your self-worth today. You are the most important person in your life. You need to look after yourself first, and then you can also take care of others.

Don't wait for someone to choose you, choose yourself

We've all failed in life. We've all applied for that job and been turned down. We've all been rejected by someone. We've all experienced someone saying no to us. Well, most of us have. But after being rejected, have you actually considered choosing yourself? Choose yourself today and you'll definitely increase your self-worth, because you'll no longer wait around for others to choose you. By choosing you, you're also teaching others to choose themselves. You are worthy of great things in life.

When I wrote my first book *Mystic Butterfly: a guide to your true self*, I sent the manuscript to almost every self-help and metaphysical publisher in the world, as well as to almost every literary agent I knew of. My hopes were high, because I fully believed in the book's message and I thought someone else would believe in it as much as I did. Unfortunately, most of the publishers and literary agents said no to me and the rest said nothing at all. This was a very long, tiring process and also disappointing, and it lowered my confidence in the book. I was sad, but at the same time, I still believed in my book. I knew that no-one else would care about my book as much as I did, being the author.

But one day, I had an inspiring idea. I thought, '*Why don't I publish my book independently?*' I then did as much research as I could to make this happen. After two years of trying to publish the book the traditional way, I'd decided to choose myself. I stopped waiting around for someone else's approval to make me an author. I chose myself, because I knew my book could help people, and the only way for this to happen was to bring it into reality instead of keeping it on my computer, along with the rejection emails. Don't get me wrong, publishing my book myself was hard work, but I was willing to accept the challenge. My sister, an amazing artist, created beautiful artwork for the book's cover. I also hired an editor, a graphic designer and a formatter who put everything together for me. Then I found a printer and a distributor to get my book out into the world, to reach as many people as possible. When the launch date arrived, I felt accomplished, happy and proud of myself, because I'd said yes to myself. I chose myself and it felt amazing.

Create your own opportunities

Are you still waiting for someone to give you permission to do something you'd like to do? Maybe you're also collecting rejection emails from publishers and literary agents, or maybe there are people around you who are telling you you're not good enough and can't succeed. Well my friend, it's time to choose yourself. Do you want to become a writer? Begin by starting a blog. Do you want to be a TV presenter, but are constantly being rejected? Don't wait any longer – create your own show and publish it on YouTube. The possibilities are unlimited. Living in this time can be difficult, but there are also many opportunities we can create for ourselves. I'm not saying you're going to be successful overnight, that people will be reading your blogs or subscribing to your YouTube channel, although that may happen. What I am saying is, stop waiting around for someone's permission and begin doing what you really want to do. If it brings you joy, do it. Keep trying, keep making mistakes, keep learning, keep doing the best you can, persevere and never give up. There are many benefits to this. I've been blogging for years and blogging has certainly improved my writing skills, and it's only now that people are actually starting to engage with my blog posts, because I've gained more skills and credibility. But imagine if I'd given up after two or three years of blogging, saying to myself, *What's the point? Nobody reads my blog anyway?* If I'd done that I wouldn't have acquired the writing skills I have now, and maybe I wouldn't have a book out or have been asked to write for the publications which approached me, who'd come across my website and liked what I'd written. If I hadn't carried on, none of this would have happened. Luckily, I said yes to myself and I continue to do so. This way, I've also connected with so many incredible people around the world and the connections and friendships we've created are amazing.

An important lessons we can learn from children

I'd like to conclude this chapter by listing a few things that we can learn from children, because they can definitely be amazing teachers. Just the other day I was sitting in the coffee shop at London Heathrow Airport. While drinking my coffee, I noticed two little boys watching the planes landing. They seemed very excited every time an aircraft touched down. They were so focused and so present in the moment, it inspired me. It made me realise how much we can learn from children, if we pay attention to them. Although I'm not a parent myself, I have a beautiful little niece and nephew, who are among my greatest teachers.

There are so many things we can learn from children, here are few:

To live more in the present moment

Children are fully present in the moment. When they're doing something, they are fully focused on it. They give their full attention to that activity and don't let anything or anyone distract them. Remember, the present moment is the only place where true life exists.

To be curious

Children ask questions. They are constantly curious about life. Curiosity is a wonderful way of being more child-like again. Let's make a decision to learn something new every day. If someone mentions something you don't know anything about, become curious about it. Pick up a book you wouldn't normally read, join a class you wouldn't normally join or simply Google something you'd like to find out more about. Do it just for fun. You never know what you may learn and how far it can take you.

To not worry

Children don't worry like we do. They don't have the same responsibilities we have, that's true, but also, they look at life differently. The same applies to teenagers and young adults. When I was learning to fly I was in my twenties. We also had much younger students at the flying school. I noticed how fearless most of them were. It was so much easier for a sixteen or a seventeen year-old to take an aeroplane for a solo flight without hesitation, than it was for a twenty-seven-year-old. I often wished I had their confidence. They weren't children anymore, but neither were they adults. But, because they worried less and didn't list all the possible things that could go wrong, they didn't talk themselves out of something they really wanted to do.

To live in a fantasy world

Albert Einstein said: *'If you want your children to be intelligent, read them fairy tales. If you want them to be more intelligent, read them more fairy tales.'* I couldn't agree more with this. Children love stories. They love playing and creating imaginary characters, and believing that they're real. I remember when I was a child, I also lived in a fantasy world, where anything was possible. This shaped my world. When I grew up, I forgot about this for a while. Luckily, I remembered it again in my late twenties. Let's awaken this precious part of our being and start believing in all that magic again.

To tell the truth

Children generally tell the truth. If they don't want to do something or they don't like someone, they say so. They say exactly how they feel. Many of us live our lives based on lies and pretending. We became good at faking smiles and saying yes when we mean no, just to be nice. We're not truthful to ourselves and others. We are often embarrassed or scared to express how we really feel. We hide behind false personas, creating lives that look good on the outside, but are painful on the inside. Let's start being more true to ourselves and others.

To not judge

Lastly, children don't judge. Religion, skin colour, nationality and many other labels don't mean anything to children. They only pick these up later from the adults around them. Can you imagine, if we judged others less, how different the future would be? No labels, no divisions, no separation, just pure love, acceptance and peace. What a wonderful thought, something only we can bring into this physical reality.

SHIFTING

It was a wintery Thursday morning. It was cold, dark and 3 am. I opened my eyes and as I didn't have to be up so early, I thought, after a few moments, I'd fall asleep again. I didn't. My mind was racing and my thoughts were overtaking the peaceful state I was trying to create. The thoughts I was having in those early hours led me to some dark places of the past, places I'd rather erase from my life completely. Once again, they seemed real, and after thinking more and more about them, I started to feel uncomfortable. So, I decided to get up. I went to the kitchen, made myself an early breakfast and got my notebook out. I began writing my thoughts down. I put the dark thoughts, full of emotion, down on the paper. I started feeling a little relief, but it wasn't enough. Later, in the shower, my feelings worsened. A distant memory flew into my mind, making me feel pain, regret and discomfort. I wondered why these thoughts were haunting me today. I had so much to do later and no time for this. By this time I was feeling angry and frustrated. It felt like a dark cloud was above my head and following me everywhere I went. Then, I realised that this must be happening for a reason. Analysing why I felt that way, that day, led me to see that I need to start a major clearing, within my life. I realised I still had so much work to do, to let some of my painful memories go.

When I returned home after a busy day of running errands, I decided to start some clearing. I began with space clearing. Cleaning my flat was a good place to start. I threw away things which needed to go, dusted the shelves, and after I'd finished I lit candles, creating a calm and peaceful atmosphere. I felt a lot better. There's certainly truth in the saying: *a clear space equals a clear mind.* Clearing the flat lifted some of the heavy energies which were floating around, but there was still something missing. After I'd cleared the visible, I needed to go even deeper and take care of the invisible. I sat on my meditation pillow, closed my eyes and took some deep breaths. Meditation always brings clarity and a fresher perspective into my life. It was difficult at first, because my mind was still jumping from place to place, but after a few minutes, the thoughts started calming down and peace began to set in. Then, a vision came into my mind. I was walking in a beautiful garden where I was surrounded by the most amazing, vivid colours. The birds were chirping and I felt the warm rays of the sun caressing my face. After a little while of walking and exploring this peaceful place, I sat down underneath a beautiful apple tree. Within a few moments, I felt so much tension melting away and leaving my body. I felt at peace with myself and everything around me. I stayed in this serene place for about twenty minutes and absorbed all these feelings of peace and beauty. When I finally opened my eyes, I felt rejuvenated. This beautiful meditation helped me to rearrange my energy and shift it from darkness into light. My unpleasant thoughts about the past didn't seem so large and upsetting anymore. I finally let them go.

Shifting higher

With that in mind, I decided to continue with more clearing for the rest of the week. It not only made me feel good, it shifted my perspective, enabling me to reach for higher thoughts and feelings. Starting a clearing process can often lead you to areas of your life which may not be flowing so well, and you realise it's finally time to do something about them. You may notice that some people in your life have been holding you back and you haven't much in common anymore. You may find that the time has come to let these people go. This may sound harsh, but, unfortunately, some people do hold us back, or we may simply have outgrown them. Being friends with someone just to be nice is being fake and untruthful. There may be people in your life you feel obliged to keep in touch with. Maybe once you had something in common, but now that's no longer the case. There may be people who drain your energy, so you avoid them, but you still call them friends. Doing so is being untrue to yourself, and to them too. Letting go of these people doesn't have to be dramatic or painful. You can let go of them gracefully. I know you care about other people's feelings, but if some friendships or a relationships aren't serving you well anymore, it's time to let them go. You can still send these people positive thoughts, but if you feel something isn't right, it probably isn't. Trust that feeling. In the last few years, I've had to say goodbye to a few people who weren't meant to share my journey with me. It was painful, but I want to be as truthful to myself and others as I can be, so it was necessary.

It's not always easy to say goodbye to the past, whatever this involves. Many people hold on to it so tightly. But why? The past is no longer here and can't be changed. You can either let it control your life, or you can let it go. Reclaim your power by letting it go and focus on the now. The past can knock on the door again and again at the most unexpected times. This is because of the imprints we've collected on our subconscious over the years, but it's up to us whether we answer the door or not.

When you feel angry...

A few years ago I did a bit of creative writing for someone. When this project was presented to me, I was instantly inspired, so I got to work almost straight away. I completed it fairly quickly too. The person I was working for was very happy with the results and so was I. Unfortunately, to this day, I haven't received any payment for the hard work I put into the project. What upset me even more was that this person disappeared completely, and became uncontactable. I'm not going to go into too much detail or talk negatively about the whole experience, however the reason I wanted to bring this up was to emphasise the lesson we're learning in this chapter, which is about shifting our perspective and not letting our past control us, whether they are our past choices or other people.

When the person didn't pay me for my work, at first I got angry. I was so angry, I couldn't focus fully on other things. I knew this had to stop and I've since made a decision not to do this anymore. I don't know what happened to this person. Maybe some tragedy had occurred in their life that I didn't know about. I decided to rise above the anger and stay neutral. For a while I did, but then the feelings of anger crept in again. My internal monologue continued: *'This is so typical, Jana. You trust everyone, and this is what happens. You should've taken an advance payment before you did the project. That's how most things get done these days. You're just too trustworthy. It's your fault.'* The more I thought about it, the angrier I felt and my frustration was building up. I knew that sooner rather than later, I'd have to take a different approach, and shift my perspective. In the end, I decided to treat this as a lesson.

A lesson learned

Instead of beating myself up again, and telling myself it was all my fault, I decided to be kind to myself. After a bad experience, we sometimes call ourselves stupid or too trustworthy and promise ourselves that we're not going to do that again. Then time passes, and yet again, we find ourselves in a similar situation. If this happens to you, you're not stupid. It's human nature to trust, and to be kind. You trusting, is only natural. Unfortunately, not everyone is honest. By being kind to yourself, and forgiving yourself for your mistake, you'll remain on a neutral frequency. Know you haven't done anything wrong. You're always learning. If a similar situation happens again, look at it as a lesson, instead of punishing yourself with harsh words. You're collecting lessons your whole life, it doesn't matter how old or experienced you are. Whatever the lesson, I'm sure it was needed to help you with your personal and spiritual growth. Anger is an emotion of limitation, and it prevents you from moving forwards in life. Anger weakens you and keeps you on a low frequency. Rising above the anger and re-focusing your attention on things which are thriving in your life is always the wiser choice. The less focus you give to your anger, the quicker it will start dissolving. Being angry never resolves anything. It only keeps you busy doing nothing, as worrying does.

After the experience which I've just discussed, I became still and listened to my inner wisdom, my intuition. I listen to it most of the time, but when my mind gets busy, it can overtake everything else, even that loving voice that says everything is going to be alright. Whenever you're making important decisions, please *check-in* with your inner voice. Your inner guidance is always there and should be acknowledged.

I must admit, I had an uneasy feeling about this person, right from the start. My intuition was trying to tell me to be careful, but I didn't listen. My mind was too involved and focused on the project. We've been trained to rely on our minds since we've been young. We're rarely told to look within. I always say to my students: *'Always ask yourself first: how do I feel about it? Not: what do I think about it?'* Asking myself how I felt about someone or something *first*, made a huge difference in my life and my experiences.

Shifting and perfectionism

I was a perfectionist from a young age. Perfectionism means setting high standards and can include the belief that things need to be done a certain way. In some ways, my perfectionism serves me well. I don't take things for granted, I'm punctual, reliable and I keep my promises. When I say I'll do something, I do it, and I do it the best way I possibly can. This has always been my strength. But, there's also a down side of being a perfectionist. It sometimes brings unnecessary pressure and anxiety into my life. I remember when I started writing and teaching, I noticed how controlling my perfectionism could be. I would find myself checking every single article dozens and dozens of times, only to find out later that there were still grammatical errors after it had been published. Similarly, I would record my meditation classes then watch them again and again, often being self-critical. This would make me edgy and feel under pressure. I'm over-careful in the way I speak and pronounce words, and I notice other people's errors, even though I know I'm not perfect myself. This can be exhausting.

Learning to shift my perspective has also meant learning to lighten up and become less of a perfectionist. As I mentioned earlier, English is not my first language. This means it will always be a little tricky to communicate when I'm tired or under pressure. At times like these, the words don't always flow as easily and effortlessly as they do when I feel good. I know it's not about the spelling or the pronunciation but about the messages I'm excited to share with others. But you can't always explain this to a perfectionist. If the perfectionist is teachable, he or she can definitely lighten up. I'm gradually letting go of some of the bad habits perfectionism taught me, by being more authentic. This way, I'm shifting more quickly, and rising above what no longer serves me. Of course, there's nothing wrong with striving for high standards. But, this is what I keep in mind now, when it comes to my work: *The people who are drawn to my work, don't come to check my grammar or to focus on the way I speak. They come because they find comfort and peace in the messages I have to share with them.* So, I'm creating, launching and learning, and keeping my perfectionism on the back seat, so it can step in, only when necessary. I keep reminding myself that nobody's perfect, to relax into everything I do and to go with the flow. I've learned now that if I waited for everything to be perfect, I'd never create anything at all. None of my articles, poems, books, music projects or videos would exist. I've made the decision to create and to launch and to learn along the way.

We're all full of inspiring ideas which are waiting to be expressed in this physical reality we live in. Don't wait to be perfect, don't hide – get your ideas out to the world. Your unique voice matters. And, if you want to make your work better, ask for feedback. I ask for feedback all the time. Some feedback can be more difficult to receive than other, but I welcome other people's opinions. It's nice to see someone else's perspective. It's a great learning experience, and it always helps me improve my work and keeps me away from perfectionism. We only see the world through our own filters and it's beneficial to be open to different points of view. At the same time, be proud of you and the work you do. You're good enough, just as you are. You have nothing to prove to anyone. Just do your best in any given moment. And, most importantly, be relaxed about it and have fun. Life is such a beautiful journey, and it's a waste of time putting extra pressure on ourselves by expecting things to be perfect and flawless. Do what makes you happy, relax and enjoy it.

I won't betray myself anymore

Have you ever betrayed yourself? What does it actually mean to betray yourself? In my understanding, it means putting other people's needs before your own, making others comfortable at your expense or always doing favours for certain people while knowing they are clearly taking advantage of you, but you still do it anyway because you haven't learned yet how to say *No*. To go even further, betraying yourself is investing your precious time and energy on people who previously let you down or didn't accept you for who you are. The list could go on and on. I'm personally tired of betraying myself. I'm also tired of seeing other amazing people be taken advantage of. Many of us, especially those who struggle, suffer in silence or are kept in the dark, are the ones who lose out or are taken advantage of. I know this because I'm still unlearning all of the above on a daily basis. I've betrayed myself far too many times, but then the day came when it was time to change that. I made a simple and clear proclamation that I wouldn't be doing this anymore. I'm sharing the proclamation in this book, because I believe to be able to shift your perception, to be who you really came here to be, you need to be able to set boundaries. Feel free to use this proclamation for yourself and to add things to it or print it out. Put it where you're going to be able to see it, daily. Let it remind you of your worth, of your truth and of the hard work you're doing.

Here is my proclamation

- I no longer betray myself by saying yes when I mean no, just for someone else's comfort

- I no longer betray myself and invest my time and energy in people who've let me down on number of occasions

- I no longer feel guilty for not responding to other people's messages or emails straight away, especially when I'm tired and need to save my precious energy

- I no longer betray myself and stay in the dark to keep others in the spotlight

- I no longer betray myself by denying my truth

- I no longer betray myself by putting myself second

- I no longer betray myself by making others comfortable, while I lose out

- I no longer betray myself and seek approval from others

- I no longer betray myself and respond to someone's social media comment if it's pushy or makes me uncomfortable, just to be nice

- I no longer invest my time in people who don't care and only contact me when they want something

- I no longer betray myself by comparing myself with others. Instead, I mind my own business, everything else is just noise

- I no longer betray myself by allowing others to take advantage of me

- I no longer betray myself by worrying too much about what others think of me

- I no longer betray myself by being drawn into other people's melodramas

Keep moving forward, keep shifting and keep staying true to yourself.

JANA PRACKOVA

CHAPTER TEN

BEING

A couple of years ago I went on a holiday to beautiful Croatia. Although the holiday was wonderful, a few things went wrong which made my energy scattered, leaving me feeling edgy, and preventing me from relaxing fully and enjoying my time off. When we arrived in Croatia, I had many things on my mind, most of which I had no control over. I found it difficult to relax. To make matters worse, in the middle of our trip, my friend, who was looking after my flat while I was away, texted me that there was a problem in the flat that required immediate attention. This really upset me, because there was little I could do, being so far away. All I could do was call a few people to deal with it, on my behalf.

A few days before our trip, I upgraded my mobile phone, online. At the time, I didn't give it a second thought, assuming it would work fine. But the process wasn't as smooth as I'd thought. I received my new phone a couple of days before the trip, but my original number wasn't transferred with it. I was told that the number would work in a couple of days, but it didn't. For the first few days of my holiday, I was on the phone to my network provider daily, without any success. So, with this, two different phone numbers and the problem in the flat, it was a bit chaotic. But then something happened. A few days before leaving Croatia, I learnt that a girl I'd been following on social media for years had lost her life in a tragic accident. I hadn't known the young woman personally, just through the internet, but I'd felt connected to her. She'd been very inspiring, and a beautiful person inside-out. At this point, I broke down and gave up.

The magnitude of this situation pushed my problems to one side. They were so insignificant, just inconveniences. I felt powerless and angry, and upset. My problems were so unimportant, compared with what had happened to this woman. She'd been only thirty-five. The lesson I learnt from this was to stop taking the little inconveniences so seriously. They can be annoying, but they can be resolved, they're not a big deal. Instead of taking our daily inconveniences so seriously, let's keep reminding ourselves of the things that truly matter. We can remind ourselves every day to be grateful for a new sunrise and a new day, and for all the amazing people in our life. Let's tell these people daily how much we love them and appreciate them. Let's be more loving and compassionate towards each other, including those we don't find it easy to connect with. Such people are also human beings, confused and scared just like us. Let's stop making a big deal of the things that don't matter and take them more lightly. Let's invest our precious energy in those things that matter most. This final chapter is focused on being. Being who you are. Being a human being who makes mistakes, who's living, breathing, learning, transforming, shifting, striving, trying, existing for a reason that's unique to you, *and* appreciating all of it.

When am I going to be truly happy?

Happiness – everyone is searching for it, but are we ever going to find it? My philosophy, however strange it may sound, is to stop searching and just be. Happy moments come and go. Happiness is a temporary state, not an ongoing thing. We can embrace the seasons of life we go through. It's easy to appreciate the times when our life blooms and the skies are blue, but we can also be patient when the dark clouds are being blown away, and we're waiting for the sun to shine again. If we were always happy, would we appreciate the joyful moments of life in the same way as we do when they come back to us, again and again? Can you relate to this way of looking at happiness? Enjoy and be grateful for the little things in life, the things you often take for granted. Gratitude can turn what you have in your life to enough. Celebrate your achievements, no matter how small. Tell yourself that you love and appreciate yourself. Do good in the world and smile at people, even without reason. It will not only shift their energy or make their day, but yours too. And most importantly, be who you are, embrace your uniqueness and your individuality. There has never been anybody like you and there's never going to be.

People who don't really know me, think I'm always about positive vibes, happiness, rainbows and butterflies. Even though I love that idea, life is somehow different in reality. I have my own struggles, bad days and negative thoughts. You've read about some of them in this book. Of course, I don't share all of my personal experiences in my books, classes or the internet, what I do instead, is talk about what I've learnt from these, to inspire and help people. Not everything is as we perceive it, not everyone is who we think they are. No-one is always happy…

…and this is one of the reasons not to compare yourself to other people

We may think that others have it 'all together' because of the way they appear to us, but the truth may be different. My own life is an example of that. The last two years have been quite tough for me, emotionally. However, I've also experienced beautiful moments of light and happiness that kept me going. People you follow online may not be exactly as you perceive them. Or, the work colleague who's always smiling, may be going through something you don't know about. Behind those false masks may be a person who is very unhappy, hurt and struggling. We've been taught to be strong and to hide our emotions, which means we're not always honest with ourselves and others, and don't always express how we really feel. I'm getting a bit tired of that, and I prefer sharing my truth with others. People want the real us, even though their perceptions may be blinded by the pretentious and the inauthentic.

What does it mean to be YOU?

'People are often unreasonable and self-centred – forgive them anyway. If you're kind, people may accuse you of ulterior motives – be kind anyway. If you're honest, people may cheat on you – be honest anyway. If you find happiness, people may be jealous – be happy anyway. The good you do today may be forgotten tomorrow – do good anyway. Give the world the best you have and it may never be enough – give your best anyway. For you see, in the end, it is between you and God. It was never been between you and them anyway.'

These powerful words by Mother Teresa are telling us to stay true to ourselves. Being true to yourself is one of the best gifts you can give to yourself.

Be kind anyway

Some time ago now I was sorting out an issue with one of the institutions I used to be a customer of. This particular issue had to be sorted in person, so one morning I walked into their office. When I arrived at Reception, it became clear that the lady at the desk hadn't had a good morning so far. She appeared a little cold, unhelpful and was also slightly rude. I felt a little upset with the way she spoke to me, but I stayed true to myself and carried on talking in a kind and understanding tone. After exchanging a few sentences, she realised that her attitude towards me wasn't working. I saw her energy change. I stayed true to myself by remaining kind and that was soon reflected back to me. The lesson that comes from this story, is to *be kind anyway*. I'm not saying, don't stand up for yourself when somebody is unpleasant to you, rude to you or has an attitude. But what you can do is defend yourself by being kind and staying true to yourself. I chose to do just that, and in the end I managed to sort an issue which had been bothering me for some time.

Create anyway

One of my favourite creative activities is writing. Sharing my thoughts about the topics I care about and strongly believe in, brings much happiness to my soul. I know not everyone reads my articles, or agrees with what I write about, or is into spirituality and personal development. That's okay. Writing makes me happy. Writing is my art and I'll continue to write anyway. And you? What is your art? Do you keep doing what makes you happy, despite other's opinions, or do you get easily discouraged by them? If it makes you happy, keep doing it.

Stay true to yourself anyway

I used to think I wasn't good enough. Therefore, I pretended I was someone else, so I could feel loved and accepted by others. I was a people pleaser, and an attention and approval seeker. You've read all about this. I learnt so many big lessons from this phase of my life. Learning to be true to myself healed many of my past wounds. It allowed me to be more accepting of myself. It taught me to love myself and nourish myself. It taught me to put myself first. No matter what, always stay true to yourself.

Sing your song anyway

Keep singing your song, keep doing what you love and what makes you happy. Never give up on your dreams, no matter how long they may take to accomplish. Keep singing your unique song because nobody can sing it the way you do. You have never happened before. Your voice is incomparable.

The truth about being Jana

Yes, I want to be inspiring. Yes, I'm excited about so many things in life. And yes, there are great things unfolding in front of me right now, but I also feel scared, tired, de-motivated, upset, unhappy and unbalanced sometimes. I cry a lot to relieve my emotional pain, but I also cry tears of joy when something works out beautifully for me. In 2018 one of my best friends passed away suddenly, and this affected my life in a great way. I miss my friend deeply, but I'm grateful that our paths crossed and I'm keeping the happy moments we shared together in my heart forever. I've been betrayed and very disappointed by some people in my life who I valued and fully trusted. But as difficult as these situations were, they made me more grateful for the people in my life who never let me down and I know I can fully rely on them. I'd always considered myself being unlucky when it came to romantic relationships, but now I'm extremely grateful for the beautiful, loving and truthful relationship I'm in today. So many things I worked so hard on didn't work out, but I'm grateful for the fantastic opportunities these redirections brought into my life. I'm *admitting* all the mistakes I've ever made. I'm *accepting* what needs to be accepted. I'm *forgiving* myself and others. I'm *healing* my past wounds as I'm stepping more into my power. I'm *transforming* my life on a daily basis by doing my best in any given moment. I'm *learning* so much along the way and I will continue to do so. I keep *creating* because this keeps me happy and fulfilled. I'm *adventuring* despite my fears. At the same time, I'm *shifting* my perspective every day. And most importantly, I'm *being* true to myself and will continue to do my best for the rest of my life. I'm enjoying the process of being courageously vulnerable.

So, as you can see my friends, life is not always about rainbows, sunshine and butterflies, but doing our best in any given moment, despite the challenges we face. They teach us a lot and help us to rise again and again – no matter where you are in your life right now, no matter what your story is, or your background, or your social status – these are just labels, labels you can rise above, simply by deciding to do so. Be true to yourself by admitting to yourself that something isn't working, something isn't flowing. Then, accept what's going on. By accepting, you're not denying your truth and you can start doing something about it. Then forgive yourself for your past mistakes. You have learned so much from them. Forgive others and let them go. Begin the process of healing your wounds. Allow these wounds to be transformed into wisdom. Keep creating that beautiful art that only you came here to create, no matter whether on a big or small scale. Keep adventuring, despite your fear. The only way to learn the lessons is to embrace your fear. Daily learning will allow you to shift to a higher level of consciousness. It's by shifting, that you can grow as a soul, as well as on a human level. And lastly, just be. Be loving, be compassionate, be courageous, be spontaneous, be hopeful, be kind, be present and most importantly, be true to yourself. Be courageously vulnerable.

EPILOGUE

It's 25th May 2021. Tomorrow is going to be a month since my precious dad very suddenly passed away at the early age of sixty-two. My heart is broken. I'm in the process of learning how to navigate through this extremely challenging time in my life and finding it very difficult. None of the challenges I've ever faced before can even compare to what my family and I are currently going through. We've been very close and the pain is very deep.

At the same time, I know my dad is with me. I feel him and I know we will meet again. This brings peace and comfort to my soul.

My dad has been an amazing dad to me and to my sister, a loving grandfather to my niece and my nephew and an incredible husband to my mum. He will remain in our hearts forever and I wanted to end this book by acknowledging him and thanking him for everything in my life.

This book was fully edited and just about ready for publishing when we suddenly lost him. With the incredible help of my loved ones, my wonderful partner and my inner guidance and strength, I found the motivation to get the book out to you, because I know my dad would've wanted that. He'd always supported me, my projects, my dreams and was my biggest fan.

Thank you again for everything, dad. I will love you forever.

Yours,
Jana xxx

ACKNOWLEDGEMENTS

Firstly, I'd like to thank my mum and dad for their love and support. You're wonderful parents. A big thank you also goes to my sister, Maria, my brother-in-law, Dusan, my niece, Adele and my nephew, Sebastian. You never let me down and I love you and appreciate you so much. And thank you to my sister, yet again, for another amazing artwork for my book cover. You always do a wonderful job.

Thank you to my boyfriend, William. You have brought so much light into my life. Thank you so much for sharing this journey with me.

I would also like to say thank you to my dearest friends Martin, Paul, Anka, Maxine, Celine, Linda and Pete. You're all very special to me and I'm so grateful that you've been part of my life for all these years.

I huge thank you also goes to Ellie, my editor, for doing a wonderful job of editing my books. I'm so glad our paths have crossed. Working with you is always a pleasure. A big thank you also goes to Jane, my graphic designer. You always do an amazing job on every project I've the pleasure to work with you on. I'm so grateful for your work.

And thank you too, dear reader. May this book bring you hope in your moments of hopelessness. May this book shine light on the parts of your life where you can see only darkness. May you see possibilities and inspiration wherever you go. And may your life be joyful and full of wonderful adventures.

With love,
Jana x

ABOUT THE AUTHOR

Jana Prackova is a spiritual life coach and meditation teacher. She is also the author of *Mystic Butterfly: a guide to your true self*, the *Mystic Butterfly Notebook* and the children's book *Aerin and a Troll*. Her mission in life is to assist others in finding their true potential, by living authentically and doing what they love.

Jana is also a private pilot and has been featured in the *LOOP* flying magazine and *The Flight School Times*, and has inspired many would-be pilots worldwide to follow their dreams.

In her spare time, she writes music and loves exploring the mysteries of the Universe.

www.mysticbutterfly.co.uk